Mike Nichols

Crumpets and Scones

Crumpets and Scones

Iris Ihde Frey

St. Martin's Press
New York

Design by Manuela Paul

Library of Congress Cataloging in Publication Data

Frey, Iris Ihde.
  Crumpets and scones.

  1. Cookery.   2. Tea.   I. Title.
TX739.F73   641.5   82-5605
ISBN 0-312-17773-9   AACR2

10 9 8 7

*For Carl
and Tom, Doug and Cliff*

Contents

Acknowledgments   x
Foreword   xi
Introduction   xiii
Standard Operating Procedures   1

I. Brewing the Perfect Cuppa   2

II. Tea with Queen Victoria   7
Crumpets/10 Strawberry Jam/11 Battenberg Cake/12
Marzipan/13 Cupid's Love Wells/14 Apricot Sugar Plums/16
Ratafias/19 Trifle/20

III. In the Gypsy Tea Room   23
Fresh Apple Cake/26 Poppyseed Cookies/27
Cigarettes Russes/28 Sweetmeats/29 Honey and Nut Puffs/30
Lips of the Beauty/32 The Lady's Navel/33

IV. High Tea   35
Rarebit/36 Cornish Pasties/37
Sally Lunn/39 Seedcake/40 Hot Cross Buns/41
Rum Nicky/42 Jumbles/43

V. Nursery Tea   45
Graham Crackers/47 Chocolate Soup/48
Tomato Sandwiches/48 Beef Tea/49 Pumpkin Buns/50
Bread and Butter Pudding/51 Brown Sugar Bears/52
Zebra Cake/53

VI. A Russian Easter Tea   55
Farina Pudding/57 Kulich/58 Pashka/59 Kisel/61

Mazurkas/63 Charlotka/64 Black Bread/66
Meringue Mushrooms/68 Candied Fruits/70

VII. Tea for Two 73
White Bread/74 Watercress Sandwiches/78
Real Cinnamon Toast/78 Cream Patties/79 Brandy Snaps/80
Love Letters/81 Trilbys/82 Chocolate Cake/84

VIII. Breakfast in Scotland 87
Oatmeal Bread/89 Orange Marmalade/90 Scots Eggs/91
Woodcock/92 Scones/92 Clotted Cream/94 Black Bun/94
Shortbread/97 Gingerbread Husbands/98 Butterscotch/99

IX. The Tea Dance 101
Sandwiches/102 Madeleines/104 Bourbon Balls/106
Cream Puffs/106 Jelly Rolls/108 Spiced Nuts/110
Fish House Punch/110 Gooseberry Fool/111

X. Hearthside Tea in an Irish Kitchen 113
Soda Bread/114 Rum Butter/115 Plum Jam/116
Porter Cake/116 Lemon Curd Tartlets/117 Boxties/119
Oatmeal Cookies/120 Yellowman/121

XI. A Garden Party 123
Fancy Sandwiches/125 Chocolate Bread/127
Vanilla Butter/128 Angel Cake/129 Rose Icing/130
Petit Fours/131 Crystallized Flowers/134 Jam Creams/135

XII. Dim Sum Tea Lunch 137
Tea Eggs/140 Buns/141 Radish Fans/143 Pot Stickers/143

Dipping Sauces/144 Date Dumplings/145
Spiced Cashews/146 Almond Jelly/147 Fortune Cookies/148

*A Few Kitchen Weights,
Measures, and Metric Equivalents*   150
Glossary of Teatime Terms   152
Varieties of Tea   155
Bibliography   156
Index   157

Acknowledgments

My great appreciation goes to these cooks who assisted with the recipes for this book: Robby and Liz Donsbach, Lois and Carrie Brunngraber, Ann Jewett, Ann Brannigan, Elizabeth Shealy, Audie Webb, Maggie Diviney, Peggy Healy, Norma Beak and Heidi Baurle.

Foreword

"Come for tea" is an invitation that promises much—comforting refreshment, friendly company, a snug kitchen setting or a fine drawing room, perhaps with a cat dozing on the hearth. But most of all, tea keeps good company with good food. This book is a collection of all those delectable treats that accompany the "taking of tea."

Turn the pages and stop for a spot of tea in Ireland, in that thatched roof cottage. Go inside where an open fireplace holds a cozy peat fire. An iron kettle on the hob is just bringing the water to a boil. Already spread on the checkered linen tablecloth is a fragrant loaf of Soda Bread, sweet Rum Butter, a bowl of Plum Jam and a platter of Boxties sizzling from the griddle. And to fill in the empty spaces, a platter of Oatmeal Cookies.

Another chapter invites you to join the children and the teddy bears for Nursery Tea. Here are recipes for such as Pumpkin Buns, Brown Sugar Bears and Chocolate Soup—tasty foods, but wholesome . . . the kind of foods that Pooh, Paddington and Alice know and love.

Or help wheel in the trolley laid with cream tea—indecently delicious confections such as Crumpets piled with fresh Strawberry Jam, Battenberg Cake and Apricot Sugar Plums.

Part the beaded curtain and enter the Gypsy Tea Room. Here tea may be sweetened with a sugar lump held between the teeth. But the main attraction is not the plate holding Honey and Nut Puffs and Sweetmeats but the tea cup itself. If you dare, dabble in the occult as you learn to read the tea leaves.

For a change, The Tea Dance. Ingredients here include slivered cucumbers (for the sandwiches), eggs and vanilla (for the

Madeleines), and potted palms (for the violinists to sit discreetly behind).

Scotch tea serves up Shortbread and Scones and the traditional, delicious Black Bun. High Tea brings out the old favorites—Cornish Pasties, Sally Lunn and Seedcake. Traveling East, sample the Easter treats in the Russian tea room or the pleasures of Dim Sum Dumplings at a Chinese tea luncheon.

Of such comforting food is this book composed—not to forget Lemon Curd Tartlets, Chocolate Bread, Gooseberry Fool, Hot Cross Buns, Jam Creams—if you think they sound good, wait until you taste them, but wait . . . I hear the tea kettle whistling.

Introduction

The notion to write this cookbook came about at a small reunion of my American family in an English tea room in Mexico City. It was a break in a day of serious sightseeing, and the good cheer of our gathering was doubled by pots of steaming tea served in flowered china cups, cakes and tarts and tasty sandwiches. Although unaccustomed to the afternoon tea ritual, we could not mistake the special contentment of the occasion.

I recalled other times and places where the world became friendlier over a cup of tea—and always there was some delectable tidbit or an extravagant assortment of pastries to accompany it. Memorable was an afternoon tea on the *Queen Elizabeth II,* shared by chance with a British dowager while we contemplated her long life, the sea around us and the seemingly endless array of cakes and tarts. Memorable, too, a simpler occasion sitting with a friend on her veranda enjoying the end-of-summer garden and home-made bread and jam.

The idea grew that food eaten with tea is endowed with a mystical ability to satisfy more than physical hunger. Whether it is sipped from paper-thin porcelain cups, a heavy earthenware mug or a glass in the Russian manner, the food served with tea has a soul-satisfying quality. Why this is so is no more easily explained than why tea has through the centuries wrapped itself in ceremony and mystery—a remarkable feat considering that, next to water, it is the cheapest beverage in the world.

The recipes in *Crumpets and Scones* were placed into particular chapters because of a certain compatibility with the other recipes; many could have been contentedly at home in other chapters. The collections of recipes within the chapters are not intended to be inflexible menus. For instance, prepared in total, the Garden Party recipes might be too elaborate for a gathering of a few old friends but not for a wedding reception.

In addition to listing recipes by name, the index groups them into categories—breads, cakes, cookies, and so on, so that the book can be used conveniently, whether to prepare a dessert for a family meal or to assemble an assortment of Christmas cookie recipes from among the Scotch, Gypsy and Victorian chapters.

It was my intention to make *Crumpets and Scones* a simply smashing sampler of teatime specialties. May the cooks who use this book find it to be as well-rounded as the cook who wrote it became while testing and tasting the recipes.

Standard Operating Procedures

Please read this page before beginning any recipes.

Ingredients

Flour: All recipes, unless they specify otherwise, use all-purpose flour.

Butter: Recipes, with a few exceptions, call for butter. Substitution of margarine or other fats, in whole or in part, is left to the discretion of the cook. Sweet butter is preferred to salted butter.

Eggs: Recipes calling for eggs have been tested using U.S. standard "Large" eggs.

Vanilla: Whenever vanilla is called for, use pure vanilla extract, not imitation.

Baking Powder: Double acting baking powder should be used. Cooks who use baking powder infrequently should test it before use to make sure it is still active. To do this, mix a teaspoon of baking powder with ⅓ cup of hot water. It should bubble vigorously.

Yeast: Manufacturers suggest that yeast be activated by combining it with "warm" water at 115 to 120 degrees. Checking this temperature on a bread-making thermometer, I found that what they call warm, I call hot.

Oven Temperature

All the recipes in this book should be baked starting with a pre-heated oven.

I

Brewing the Perfect Cuppa

The brewing of tea is a simple but satisfying ritual. Anyone who has never done more than slosh a tea bag in a cup of water may look forward to becoming part of this worthy tradition.

A tale is told of a young nun in a convent long ago in Japan who served tea to visitors. When they asked if the tea had been made from rainwater the nun expressed amazement at their ignorance. She explained that she had used water from snow collected from the Temple plum trees. It had filled a blue jar and lay buried under the earth for five years. She asked how they could expect rainwater to possess such clarity and lightness. It is not necessary to seek such rare water to make good tea. And whether served from cups of white jade or heavy mugs it is within the reach of all who are guided by the following simple steps.

1. "Hot the Pot." Pour hot water into the teapot and let it sit while bringing fresh tap water to boil in a kettle.

2. As kettle is about to boil, empty teapot and measure into it one teaspoonful of tea per cup plus the mandatory "one for the pot." Bring the pot to the kettle, never the kettle to the pot. The water must be at a full rolling boil to release the full flavor from the leaves but should not be allowed to continue boiling or it will become flat.

3. Pour boiling water over the tea leaves. Put the lid on the pot, cover with a tea cozy and steep for 5 minutes.

If the teapot has an effective built-in strainer, pour directly into the cup. If not, pour into cup through a strainer. If all the tea is not to be served immediately, pour off the brewed tea into a separate heated pot as continued steeping will make it taste heavy and bitter.

To make stronger tea, increase the amount used rather than lengthening the brewing time. Strength of tea cannot be judged by color—some teas brew up very lightly. A teapot filled with hot water standing by may be used to dilute the brew to the guest's preference. Directions for making good iced tea are given in the Garden Party chapter.

All tea belongs to the same evergreen plant of the camellia family yet it has as many faces and character differences as another beverage—wine. The uniqueness of tea comes from the climate, the altitude and the soil where it is grown and from the manner of its harvesting and methods of processing.

There are three resulting types of tea—green, brown, called oolong, and black. Black tea is fully oxidized, making a dark hearty brew when steeped. Oolong is partly oxidized, turning it to a half brown, half green color. Green tea is not oxidized. Leaves from the same tea plant processed to these three stages would taste distinctly different from each other.

Most tea is sold in blends that the various importers have developed for taste and standards of consistency. The name Orange Pekoe so commonly seen on the tag of a tea bag actually is a grading name for the size of the leaves but it has come to stand for the every day common cup of tea.

Getting to know the many tastes of tea is a fine adventure. There is the geography—teas come from China, India, Ceylon, Indonesia, Japan, Taiwan, even from Africa and South America. There is the challenge of developing the ability to taste the differences which have been described as winy, smoky, fruity, flowery and so on. There is an appreciation of the differences in color and the many aromas. Each chapter has suggestions for specific teas that go especially well with the food and the occasion.

To dispel any uncertainties that may linger about the serving or the taking of tea, here is a brief run-through. At a small party, when the guests number a dozen or less, the hostess or host prepares and pours the tea while seated at a table with a tea cup and saucer for each guest within reach. A large tray holds all the trappings for brewing the tea. There is a teapot large enough to hold at least one cup of tea for each guest's first serving. There may be what is called, even in the best of circles, a slop basin. This holds the discarded hot water that was used to warm the teapot. There is a caddy or two filled with tea. In former days it was usual to ask the guest's preference for tea from China or India, so there would be a teapot for each. As boiling water in a kettle will not endure the trip from the kitchen stove, a spirit lamp, also called an alcohol burner, is used at the tea table. To speed up the heating, the kettle may be brought almost to the boil at the kitchen stove and then transferred. A samovar or an electric urn also provides boiling water at the tea table. The tea leaves, placed in the pot, are deluged with boiling water from the kettle. The lid is replaced and the teapot may be covered with a cozy while it steeps. When it is ready, the hostess asks, "Sugar? One lump or two?" and so sugar tongs are another item of the equipage. The next question is, "Milk or lemon?" If the answer is milk, one must face the controversy of whether the milk is poured into the cup before or after the tea. Those who feel most intensely about the issue believe that the scalding of the milk as the tea pours over it adds a finer flavor. Milk is used, not cream. For those who prefer clear tea there is a plate holding lemon slices and a lemon fork. There may also be a teapot containing very hot water to dilute tea for those who like a weaker brew.

At the other end of the table or on a nearby table—or on a tiered curate standing by, are the breads and cakes and cookies. Plates, each with a folded napkin on top, are stacked waiting for the guests to help themselves. If jam and butter are being served, small knives will be set out, but there will be forks only if the cakes served cannot be managed without.

If a larger number of guests are invited, the hostess asks a friend to pour. This assignment carries with it a degree of prestige as the hostess will have asked a very dear friend, a person with social grace and charm or a great beauty—or perhaps, all three in one.

Guests may pull up a chair to the serving table and sit there to drink a cup of tea and chat until another guest arrives, or they may be seated about the room. Afternoon teas don't have tables set with places—it is a time to perch or circulate while practicing the fine art of balancing cup and saucer, plate and napkin. For the hostess, the preparation and serving of tea is perhaps the most theatrical and charming role she may ever encounter.

II

Tea with Queen Victoria

Crumpets
Strawberry Jam
Battenberg Cake
Marzipan
Cupid's Love Wells
Apricot Sugar Plums
Ratafias
Trifle

Queen Victoria, in all her royal rotundity, personified her era's passion for sweets. In her diary and in letters she made frequent resolutions to eat less: "Only half a biscuit for luncheon." But she was *largely* unsuccessful. A succession of superb cooks whom she employed followed the policy that more is better and too much is not enough. They delighted in creating elaborate, ornate pastries and desserts. Two of her cooks wrote big, popular cookbooks giving precise descriptions of those tasty dishes fit to set before a queen. But the Queen also enjoyed cooking treats for her beloved Prince Albert in their private kitchen and the majority of recipes from her own collection are for sweets and confections.

Beginning with a scrapbook she kept as a young girl, she copied recipes handed down to her from court circles. There are homely hints that any housewife might have saved: "An Old Receipt for Barley Water—a sure cure for the cold if served hot." Another, for a cake that will keep for a quarter of a year, was titled "A Cake That Will Not Moulder." But more often there were recipes that may have appealed to her because of her penchant for ornamentation. One was a dessert called Moonshine. Preparations began by boiling two calf's feet to make a gelatin, and ended after considerable effort when a half-moon mold and several star molds were set into a round basin and filled separately with tinted custards. An icing recipe called for the whites of 24 eggs to be whisked well for three or four hours. Cherries in any form were another of Victoria's favorites. For her coronation banquet she requested a cherry tart—and had second helpings lavishly topped with whipped cream.

The Queen loved her tea. An advertisement on the back cover of an 1897 *Ladies Home Journal* featured a photograph of the Queen sitting with President McKinley. In the background a handsome white-turbaned Indian holds a tray with two tea cups. The caption, "The Regal Beverage," is followed by: "Mr. President, may I offer you a cup of pure tea from Ceylon and India?" During Victoria's reign the East Indian Company had controlled the world's tea supply until the American-designed Clipper Ships shrank the size of the globe. The Clippers, under their spread of snow-white canvas, said to be the loveliest ever to sail the oceans, were built for tea's transport. The tea races, ships speeding home from China with the first of the new season's tea, were for a generation an exciting annual event. A fortune could be made by betting on the outcome—and another fortune from the cargo. Telegrams were sent from checkpoints and the race's progress was followed as anxiously as ticker tapes are today.

Tea at the palace was served from the Queen's favorite ornate silver tea service. It is still in use today at Buckingham Palace, although there is general consensus among British subjects that a china or crockery teapot makes better tea than any kind of metal—including royal sterling silver. Liveried footmen would roll in the trolleys and the butler would pour—except for a family tea, when the Queen poured. A hundred years later, the present Queen follows teatime ritual religiously each afternoon, replacing "Shall I pour?" with the well-worn but endearing, "Shall I be Mum?"

There is little question as to what kind of teas Queen Victoria, as Empress of India and Ceylon, brewed in the royal teapot. Today, there are several named blended teas that have since proved to be court favorites. Often they are packed in decorative tin caddies. Some of the famous blends are: Queen Mary's (by permission of the late Queen), Coronation Tea, Lady Londonderry and Royal Blend. Demerara sugar which was used then to sweeten tea is very much like today's raw sugar—large crystals of a brownish color. And surely, a pitcher of milk for the tea will be standing by.

A white damask cloth, the folds ironed in, or anything heavy with lace will be most appropriate, as will mother-of-pearl-handled spoons and a bamboo curate to hold the waiting foods. If china patterns don't match, so much the better; the Queen loved to see pattern piled upon pattern.

Here follow recipes for an extravagant royal Victorian tea chosen to express a delight in excess. No guest will sample them all but all guests will sample some.

Crumpets

Nothing sounds more English than tea and crumpets. A sort of flat muffin riddled with yeasty holes, the crumpet is served warm from the griddle and then, ideally, toasted on a long fork over an open fire. And always crumpets are described as being awash with melting butter and strawberry jam. Because they are made from batter, they require rings of some sort during the baking process. Traditional crumpet rings are 4 inches across. Three-inch substitutes may be made from clean tuna cans with tops and bottoms removed. Even smaller rings—such as cookie cutters—or ones formed from heavy aluminum foil may be more suitable for today's appetites. A Scandinavian pancake skillet with round depressions works perfectly for making smaller crumpets.

> ¼ cup warm water (115 degrees)
> 1 package dry yeast
> 1 teaspoon sugar
> ½ cup milk, scalded and cooled to lukewarm
> 1 egg
> 1½ cups flour
> ¼ teaspoon salt
> 2 tablespoons butter, melted

Combine the warm water, yeast and sugar in a mixing bowl and let set for 10 minutes.

Add the milk and egg and mix well. Add the flour, salt and butter and beat vigorously until batter is smooth. An electric mixer works fine—the beating encourages the holes to form.

Cover the bowl with a towel and set in a warm draft-free place for an hour or more or until batter has doubled in size. Stir batter to deflate it.

Heat a skillet to moderate heat. Arrange the well-buttered rings on the skillet and let them warm up. Drop a heaping tablespoon of batter into each ring. When crumpets begin to bubble and bottoms are lightly brown, remove rings, turn crumpets and brown the second side. Serve hot from skillet. Makes about a dozen.

Strawberry Jam

Favorite consort to crumpets is red jam, especially strawberry jam. Here is a scaled-down recipe that can be made quickly and eaten quickly, thus eliminating the need for sterilizing and sealing jars. Because strawberries are so low in pectin, two boosters have been included in the ingredients—lemon juice and powdered pectin. They will prevent the finished jam from being too runny. Also, using them means the jam can be cooked quickly, preserving the bright red color of the fresh strawberries.

> 1 pint basket of strawberries (about 3½ cups)
> 1¼ cups sugar
> 1 tablespoon lemon juice
> 2 tablespoons powdered pectin

Use only perfect berries. Rinse and drain and dry. If they are large, cut in half and place in a large, heavy stainless or enameled pan over moderate heat. Cover berries with the sugar and add lemon juice. Stir lightly until mixture turns pink and juicy. Stop stirring (stirring prevents the heat from rising quickly and longer cooking sacrifices the bright color and firm texture of the berries). Raise heat to high. When the mixture begins to boil vigorously, set timer for 15 minutes. A candy thermometer inserted in the jam should register 220 degrees at the end of 15 minutes. Sprinkle pectin over jam and stir it in. Let it boil for a minute. Remove jam from heat and leave undisturbed for 10 minutes.

Pour into a pint-sized preserve jar or into a fancy jam jar. If strawberries congregate at the top, stir them after cooling awhile to distribute evenly.

Battenberg Cake

This is a true Victorian fancy—a checkerboard of pink and yellow cake held together with apricot jam and wrapped in a case of Marzipan. It is at the same time a rich delicacy and an ornate artistic creation. Little wonder that it was a favorite of the Queen. World War I caused the name Battenberg to be changed to Mountbatten—but the cake is still known in "the old way."

> ½ cup butter
> 1 cup sugar
> 4 eggs
> 1 teaspoon vanilla
> 2 cups flour
> 2 teaspoons baking powder
> Red and yellow food coloring
> ½ cup apricot jam

Prepare the baking pan. Use heavy-duty foil to divide an 8-inch square baking pan in half. Fold foil several times to create a divider the length and height of the pan. It will be supported by the stiff dough—pink on one side and yellow on the other. Butter pan bottom well. Have all ingredients at room temperature before starting.

Cream together the butter and sugar until light and fluffy. Gradually beat in the eggs. Add vanilla and 4 drops of yellow food coloring. Sift flour with baking powder and fold into mixture gently.

Divide mixture in half. To one portion add 5 or 6 drops of red food coloring to tint it a pale pink. (Color deepens during baking.) With spatula, smooth batters into divided pan, yellow on one side, pink on the other. Bake in 375 degree oven for 30 minutes or until cake tester inserted in center comes out dry. Cool for 5 minutes before turning cake out onto rack.

When completely cool, slice each cake lengthwise down the center. Trim away crusts remaining on tops and sides. Warm apricot jam and strain it. Place a yellow cake strip next to a pink strip. Use a pastry brush to spread apricot jam generously to join the two strips. Repeat with the remaining two strips. Spread the top of one joined cake with jam and place the second joined cake on top, placing pink on yellow and vice versa. Save remaining jam to spread on outside of cake later. Wrap cake tightly in plastic wrap and place in refrigerator while preparing Marzipan. May be cut into 12 or more slices.

Marzipan

Originally called Marchpane, this ground almond and sugar comfit has long been a court favorite.

> 1 cup almonds, blanched
> 1 cup confectionery sugar
> 1 tablespoon water
> ½ teaspoon almond extract
> 1 egg white
> Yellow food coloring

In a processor or blender, grind almonds and sugar until powdered. Add water, almond extract, egg white and a drop or two of yellow food coloring. Blend until a soft paste is formed. Refrigerate until paste firms.

Measure the length, sides and top of the Battenberg Cake and roll Marzipan out to these dimensions. Dust rolling pin and board with confectionery sugar if paste is sticky.

Coat top and two long sides of the cake with warmed apricot jam. Drape Marzipan over and press on. Trim both ends. Refrigerate until serving time. Makes 1 cup.

Cupid's Love Wells

Charles Francatelli wrote, "the Greatest honor to which he could aspire, to have served as Chief Cook and Maitre-d'Hotel to Her Most Gracious Majesty the Queen." He was a most inventive cook. For example, here is his description of one of his triumphs, Savoy Cake in the form of a Glazed Ham. After sculpting the cake with a sharp knife, "that part of the rind which is usually left adhering to the knuckle as an ornament must be imitated by spreading a layer of chocolate icing over it, in the form of a scallop shell; the remaining part of the surface of the ham should be masked with a coating of diluted bright apricot jam, to imitate glaze." After filling the cake with jellied fruit or cream, he instructed, "Place the ham on its dish, fix a handsome paper ruffle on the knuckle with a small silver skewer; garnish the ham round the base with croutons of some kind of sweet jelly, pink and white; place an ornament of the same on the top, and serve." An incredible edible.

Francatelli had a picturesque way of noting kitchen weights and measures. "Roll dough to the thickness of a penny," he would instruct. "Cut circles the size of a shilling. Make biscuits twice the size of a five-shilling piece and wafers cut to the size of a half-crown piece. Stamp out puff paste rings the size of a shilling. Throw in as much salt as will stand on a sixpence, as much nutmeg as will hold on a half-penny." What a picture the chef must have made, cheeks rosy from the ovens, his pockets ajingle with the many coins he needed to do his job.

He was chef during the golden honeymoon years. For the blushing bride (and Victoria had an entry in her receipts on the becomingness of blushing) here in his own words are the directions for a favorite cherry tart. (The Puff Paste is available in grocery store freezer cases. Thaw according to package directions.)

8 ounces Puff Paste
Yolk of 1 egg
Cherry jam

Roll out half a pound of puff paste to the thickness of the sixth part of an inch; stamp out about 18 circular pieces from this with a fluted tin cutter, 1½-inch in diameter, and place these in rows on a baking sheet previously wetted to receive them. Then, stamp out as many more pieces with a smaller fluted cutter only 1-inch in diameter, and after stamping out the center of these, wet the surface of the others over with a paste-brush, and lay one of the smaller ones on each of the others; press them down with the fingers, egg over the tops, and bake them a bright light color; when they are nearly done, shake some sugar over them with the dredger, put them back again into the oven for a minute or two, and then pass the red-hot salamander over them to give them a bright glossy appearance. Previously to serving these Love's Wells, fill them either with preserved cherries, greengage jam, or currant jelly. Makes 18.

Apricot Sugar Plums

This confection is made of two hollowed cookies enclosing a "pit" made of the crumbs, chocolate and jam. They may then be glazed and blushed and finished with a clove for a stem, making a very realistic "Apricot." In Victorian times they were arranged in a pyramid on a silver compote, encircled with shiny green leaves. A second bonus cookie comes with it—extra crumb mixture becomes brandy balls.

Cookies

1 cup sugar
1 teaspoon baking powder
¾ cup milk, heated
½ teaspoon vanilla
⅔ cup vegetable oil
¼ cup flour
2 eggs, lightly beaten
4 cups flour

Stir sugar and baking powder together in a large bowl and then stir in warmed milk. Stir in vanilla, vegetable oil and ¼ cup of flour. Add the lightly beaten eggs, stir well and set aside for one hour.

At the end of the hour, gradually beat 4 cups of flour into the mixture. It will be stiff, much like a soft bread dough. With a teaspoon take heaping spoonfuls and with well-buttered hands roll each into a round ball. Place balls on buttered baking sheets. There should be approximately 48 balls.

Bake in 350 degree oven for 15 minutes. Cookies will be light colored. Take one out to test doneness. With a small, sharp knife, cut a circle from the flat bottom, then continue to cut and scrape out the center of the cookie until a shell remains. If the center is not baked through, bake the cookies a few minutes longer.

Remove centers from all cookies while still warm, reserving all crumbs. Place hollowed shells on rack to cool.

Filling

Crumbs from cookie centers
½ cup walnuts, chopped
1 cup apricot jam
3 ounces sweet baking chocolate, melted
⅛ cup apricot brandy (or rum)

Place the crumbs from centers into a blender or processor and spin until they are finely ground.

Combine walnuts, apricot jam and melted chocolate. Add the cookie crumbs and mix well. Add apricot brandy and stir. If the mixture is too dry to hold together, add more brandy by the teaspoonful.

Take the cookie shells from the racks and beginning with the largest, pair them off by size into mates. From the crumb mixture roll a ball big enough to fill the insides of the two halves. Put the "pit" in one half. (Use extra crumb mixture to roll into brandy balls. They may be eaten "as is" or rolled in granulated or confectionery sugar or cocoa. Makes about 18.)

Cookie Glue

1 egg white
1 teaspoon cream of tartar
½ cup confectionery sugar

With an electric mixture, beat egg white with cream of tartar until stiff. Gradually beat in the sugar. Beat for 10 minutes. Or blend for a few minutes in blender or processor. Keep plastic wrap over bowl while storing to prevent crust from forming. With finger spread a fine ring of glue around the empty cookie half. Fit it onto the filled half and press them together. Place cookies on racks and let dry until fixed.

Glaze
½ cup confectionery sugar
2 tablespoons water
Yellow and red food coloring
Whole cloves

When cookie halves have dried together, stir sugar into a smooth paste while slowly adding water. Add three drops of yellow and one drop of red food coloring to tint glaze a pale apricot color. With a pastry brush coat a thin glaze all over Apricots. When glaze has dried use a small skewer or a toothpick to make a hole in the top of each where the stem would be. In each hole insert a whole clove. To leftover glaze add another drop or two of red food coloring. With fingertip "paint" a blush on the Apricot. Candied or fresh mint leaves may be added for more realism. Serve on a lace doily or a bed of shiny green leaves. Makes about 24 cookies.

Ratafias

Ratafias, a common "biscuit" in the Victorian household, were usually purchased ready-baked. Although Chef Francatelli frequently used them as an ingredient in his creative concoctions, he did not include a recipe for them in his encyclopedic collection of recipes numbering in the thousands. "Procure Ratafias" were his instructions—much as today's cookbooks call for store-bought phyllo leaves or puff pastry. Mrs. Beeton, the Julia Child of the last century, did give a recipe, but only reluctantly, saying, "We think it almost or quite as economical to purchase such articles as these at a good confectioner's." Times change. Lacking good confectioners, we pass on her recipe with one adjustment. Mrs. Beeton calls for a quarter of the almonds to be bitter—even though she had previously noted that bitter almonds should be used with caution since "four drops of their essential oil have caused the death of a middle-sized dog."

> 1 cup almonds, blanched
> ¾ cup sugar
> 2 egg whites

Grind almonds very fine. (If using a processor or blender to grind nuts, include the sugar in the container as it will keep the nuts dry and prevent their oil from surfacing. Thanks be to the Industrial Revolution.)

Whip egg whites very stiff. Blend the almond and sugar mixture gently into the egg whites. Place mixture in a pastry bag and pipe button-sized rounds onto baking sheets lined with paper or foil. Bake them in a 300 degree oven for 10 minutes. Makes about 5 dozen small Ratafias.

Trifle

An assemblage of sponge cake spread with jam and sprinkled with spirits, enfolded with custard and crowned with whipped cream—more logically called Significant than Trifle. The name evolved from Tipsy Cake, its less grand predecessor. Queen Victoria's circa 1850 recipe calls for four kinds of jam—apricot, greengage, strawberry and orange—and three kinds of spirits— Madeira, brandy and curaçao. Just to contemplate it is to gain five pounds! Contemporary versions limit the choice to raspberry jam and sherry. Assembling the rich ingredients in a footed crystal trifle bowl has been known to send cooks into a frenzy of improvisation—trimming with mosaics of gelatin, almonds, crushed ratafias, glacé cherries, candied angelica and other comfits. More practical cooks merely consider Trifle a good way to use up stale cake. Here is a version of Trifle that should endure well into the 21st century.

    2 cups milk
    ⅓ cup sugar
    1½ tablespoons cornstarch
    2 eggs
    1 teaspoon vanilla
    1 layer sponge cake (halve the Jelly Rolls recipe, page 108,
        and bake in a 9-inch round cake pan. Or use lady fingers.)
    4 tablespoons raspberry jam
    ¼ cup sweet sherry
    1 cup pears, sliced (canned or freshly poached)
    1 cup whipping cream

Heat milk in the top of a double boiler over direct heat just until the surface develops a film. Do not allow it to boil. In a mixing bowl stir sugar, cornstarch and eggs together. Add a little of the hot milk to the mixture very slowly, stirring vigorously. Gradually add remainder of milk, stirring all the while. Transfer back to top of double boiler and cook over (but not in) hot but not boiling water until the mixture thickens, stirring constantly. Remove from heat and add vanilla. Cover tightly with plastic wrap and set aside to cool.

Slice sponge cake crosswise into two layers. Spread the uncut side of each with raspberry jam. Cut the layers into wedges and line a glass bowl with some of them—jam side against the glass—arranging them evenly with space between wedges. Sprinkle half of the sherry over the cake. Fill spaces with some of the custard. Place more cake slices in the bowl, alternating them over the first layer. Reserve a few slices for finishing the top. Sprinkle the rest of the sherry over the second layer of cake. Pour the remaining custard over the cake. Arrange pear slices in a spoke design over custard.

Whip cream until stiff and pile it on top of custard and pears. Some of the whipped cream may be reserved to pipe designs of rosettes from a pastry bag. Finish the top with the remaining sponge cake cut into strips or triangles. Decorate with ratafias or macaroons, candied violet petals or glacé cherries if desired. Chill until served. Makes about 10 servings.

III

In the
Gypsy Tea Room

Fresh Apple Cake
Poppyseed Cookies
Cigarettes Russes
Sweetmeats
Fruit and Nut Balls, Chocolate Gold
Honey and Nut Puffs
Lips of the Beauty
The Lady's Navel

Part the beaded curtain the better to view the tea table set for a interlude of intrigue. A paisley-print cloth is spread, its fringe fairly dripping to the floor. Lavishly set under plates are gilded paper doilies. To nibble on, before the serious business of fortune telling begins, there are treats both sweet and soothing. A lacquered box holds a cache of Sweetmeats, the better to enclose their aromatic spices. When a tambourine is passed it is found to be filled with a seductive sweet—Lips of the Beauty. One plate holds the treats some call the Lady's Navel (referred to by others as Belly Buttons). Another plate holds Apple Cakes baked with charms and magical ingredients and tied around with red ribbon—the ultimate sorcery for obtaining luck in love. A dish of apples sits ready to prophesy fate in love. If an apple can be cut in two without slicing a seed, the wish of the heart will be fulfilled.

Tea cups must be white, shallow, wide at the top and have a smooth interior. The teapot must be the type without a built-in strainer or tea may be brewed directly in the cup. Quality tea is a must—cheaper grades are too fragmented to be read. Yunnan, a fragrant black tea from a southern province in China, is a good choice. To brew the tea, place a scant teaspoonful of leaves in the cup and fill it with boiling water. The leaves will settle to the bottom.

Gypsies share with the Russians the custom of sweetening tea by sipping it through a sugar cube held between the teeth. Milk and lemon are not offered as they might cloud the prophecy.

When only a few drops of tea remain, the reader takes the cup and swirls the liquid around several times to spread the leaves against the sides. Then the cup is turned upside down onto the saucer to drain remaining tea while a count of seven is made aloud. Turn the cup up and read.

The reading must not be hurried. The cup must be turned and studied from all directions. What at one glance appears to be a ground hog may actually be an upside down yacht.

The placement of the symbols in the cup is significant: leaves on the bottom foretell the distant future; the sides, events not too far off; the rim area, events imminent.

Lucky symbols are triangles, stars, clover, anchors, trees, flowers, arches, bouquets and crowns. Ominous symbols are coffins, crosses, snakes, rodents, umbrellas, hourglasses, steeples and owls. It must be remembered that symbols which are large or very clear have more strength than others. Symbols may be read in a single leaf or formed by a cluster.

The language of the leaves has been practiced for three centuries, during which time the following interpretations have been proved to be correct.

Anchor—success in business

Angel—good news

Arch—a journey, possible honeymoon

Arrow—distressing news

Axe—difficulties overcome

Bouquet—luckiest symbol, fulfillment of desires

Circle—a wedding, gifts

Fruits—if in season, contentment

Heart—love, in marriage

Horseshoe—good luck, prosperity

Kite—long journey

Lines—advancement, long life

Moon—romantic involvement

Mushroom—separation, business or personal

Scissors—separation

Square—comfort, a letter

Star—health and wealth

Tree—wishes will come true

Triangle—unforseen legacy

ANIMALS

Bear—anticipated danger through stupidity

Birds—if flying good news, if not, a journey

Butterfly—anticipated pleasure

Cat—treachery if in bottom of cup, otherwise, domestic bliss

Crawling insects—alarming gossip

Dog—faithful friends

Frog—romantic conquest

Lion—powerful, influential friends

Pig—faithful lover, envious friends

Rabbit—an absent friend requires help

If no symbols are evident or if too few leaves have remained in the cup, it is the fault of the seeker who has not concentrated or is in an indecisive state of mind. Explain this to the seeker, pour another cup of tea and try again. If necessary, refer to the following all-purpose fortunes.

All Purpose Fortunes

1. You will receive an important letter.
2. A person of the opposite sex endowed with great wealth and beauty is about to enter your life.
3. You have twice missed a treasure but will have a third opportunity.

Fresh Apple Cake

This recipe is included not because it is delicious but because it is full of potent portents. Just one bite is said to be enough to bewitch the unwary taster. For the cook who dares, these further steps may be taken. On St. George's Day, April 23rd, collect a handful of flower petals and a teaspoonful of dew and add to the batter. To further facilitate the action of the charm, bake coins into the cake. And finally, tie each piece of cake round with a red ribbon to assure luck in love. And that's no flimflam!

¼ cup butter
1 cup sugar
1 teaspoon vanilla
1 egg
2 cups well-chopped apples
1 cup flour
½ teaspoon baking powder
½ teaspoon baking soda
1 teaspoon cinnamon
½ teaspoon ground cloves
½ cup chopped walnuts

In one bowl beat together in the following order butter, sugar, vanilla and egg. Stir in chopped apples (3 large or 4 medium apples make about 2 cups chopped). In another bowl sift together flour, baking powder and soda, cinnamon and cloves. Stir in walnuts. Combine the two mixtures and blend together well. Pour into a greased 8-inch square pan. Bake in 350 degree oven for 45 minutes. Allow to cool in pan for 10 minutes, then turn out to cool on rack. Cut into nine squares.

Poppyseed Cookies

The original recipe begins, "First steal a chicken. When it lays an egg. . . ." This is a gypsy treat that, when bitten into, bites back—polka-dotted as the cookies are with crunchy poppyseeds. They are not too sweet and have a wholesome, earthy quality.

> ⅓ cup evaporated milk or cream
> ⅓ cup poppy seeds
> ¾ cup flour
> ⅓ cup sugar
> 1 teaspoon baking powder
> 1 pinch salt
> 1 teaspoon ground coriander
> 1 egg

Heat milk, stir in poppyseeds and set aside to cool. Meanwhile, combine flour, sugar, baking powder, salt and coriander and sift twice. Break egg carefully into small bowl and remove about 1 teaspoon of the white, reserving it for later use as glaze. With a fork beat the yolk and remaining white and add to the lukewarm milk and poppyseed mixture. Add to dry ingredients, blending thoroughly. Drop from teaspoon onto greased cookie sheet. Bake in 350 degree oven for 8 to 10 minutes. Turn oven to broil for a minute or two, watching carefully so cookies don't get too brown. Remove from oven and immediately dip just the top of each cookie into the reserved egg white to glaze them. Makes abour 2 dozen cookies.

Cigarettes Russes

These cylinder-shaped cookes are formed by rolling the round cookie—hot from the oven—around a wooden pencil. They have the texture of a very crisp wafer but the flavor of rich chocolate brownies. Passed to guests in a silver cigarette box, they present no threat to health.

2 egg whites
½ cup sugar
¼ cup butter, melted
½ teaspoon vanilla
1½ tablespoons flour
1 teaspoon cocoa

Put egg whites in a small bowl and beat with a fork until frothy. Add sugar and beat until smooth. Stir in the melted butter, vanilla, flour and cocoa.

Using a buttered and floured baking sheet spoon out scant tablespoonsful of batter. With the back of the spoon smooth each into a 3 × 4 inch rectangle. (Try 1 or 2 cookies at first to test baking time and technique. If cookies harden before they can be rolled return baking sheet to oven for a few minutes.) Bake at 350 degrees for 8 minutes. Remove from oven and let cool for a few seconds. Using a metal spatula to peel cookie from pan, roll tightly around a wooden pencil. Remove to a rack and cool, seam down. Makes about one dozen.

Sweetmeats

The ingredients for Sweetmeats should ideally be gathered barefoot and with golden earrings ajangle from among the hedgerows and woods. If obtained from the grocer's shelf, be as free as a gypsy in adding or subtracting fruits and nuts according to preference, seasonal availability or that which is sale-priced.

Fruit and Nut Balls
½ cup walnuts
2 tablespoons sugar
1 small orange
1 pound prunes, pitted
½ cup grated coconut
Sugar

Put walnuts and 2 tablespoons sugar into blender, processor or grinder and spin until nuts are coarsely chopped. Remove from container. Put orange, seeded and cut into eighths, into container with prunes. Process them—in several batches if necessary—until both fruits are uniformly chopped. Combine nuts, fruit mixture and coconut until blended. Roll into a log and cut into 1-inch pieces. Form each into a ball. Roll in granulated sugar. Makes 1 dozen.

Chocolate Gold
1 cup golden raisins
1 cup dried apricots
Grated rind of a lemon
4 ounces bittersweet chocolate, melted
2 teaspoons brandy
Confectionery sugar

Coarsely chop raisins and apricots in blender or processor. Add lemon rind, melted chocolate and brandy and mix well. Form into a long narrow log and cut into 1-inch squares. Coat each cube with confectionery sugar. Makes 1 dozen.

Honey and Nut Puffs

A version of baklava—that sweet made with paper-thin leaves of pastry available in freezer cases as phyllo dough. These are made as individual Puffs to eat without a fork instead of being baked in a sheet pan and cut into the usual diamond shapes. It's true that these triangular Puffs are sticky, but they're finger-licking good.

½ pound phyllo pastry, defrosted
½ cup butter, melted and kept warm

Filling
1 cup walnuts, ground
½ cup blanched almonds, ground
2 tablespoons sugar
1 teaspoon cinnamon
¼ teaspoon ground cloves

Mix the nuts with the sugar, cinnamon and cloves.

Remove thawed phyllo leaves or sheets from wrappings, unfold and cover them with a damp towel. Work with one sheet at a time. With a wide pastry brush spread the sheet with a light coating of the melted butter. Fold lengthwise in half two times, coating each layer with butter as it is folded. Place a generous tablespoon of the nut mixture on the pastry. Fold the pastry strip up in triangles as a flag is folded. Brush the top with butter. Place Puffs near to each other in a baking pan and bake at 375 degrees for 15 minutes or until they turn a golden color. While Puffs are baking prepare syrup.

Syrup
1 cup water
1 cup sugar
1 cinnamon stick
3 whole cloves
¼ cup honey
½ lemon

In deep saucepan combine water, sugar, cinnamon stick, cloves and honey and bring to a boil. Squeeze the juice from the lemon into the pan. Cut the lemon rind into a few pieces and add to the pan. Reduce heat so that syrup is barely boiling and cook for 5 minutes. Remove from heat and skim off the froth. Remove stick cinnamon, cloves and lemon rind. Pour all or part of the syrup, depending on sweetness desired, over the Puffs. Leftover syrup is delicious on waffles or pancakes. Before serving transfer individual Puffs to a serving dish. Makes about 16.

Lips of the Beauty

A plateful of lips, one shaped into a Mona Lisa smile, another mysterious and veiled, another—thanks to a good measure of leavening—swollen into a petulant pout. The final touch for the Beauties, lip gloss, is provided by a sprinkling of red sugar. Spicy with cardamon and a pinch of pepper, they might be called hot lips.

2 tablespoons butter
1 tablespoon sugar
½ cup honey
2 tablespoons cold water
1½ cups flour
1 teaspoon baking soda
¼ teaspoon salt
½ teaspoon cardamon
⅛ teaspoon white pepper

Mix butter, sugar and honey thoroughly. Beat in water. Stir flour, baking soda, salt, cardamon and pepper together until blended. Stir into butter mixture. Pat dough into a flat rectangle on plastic wrap and chill in refrigerator for 2 hours or overnight.

Roll dough to ⅓ inch thickness. A heart-shaped cookie cutter is used to form the lips. Stamp along edges of dough leaving the bottom third of the cutter extending beyond the dough. This will form a heart with the point missing. Transfer to lightly greased baking sheet. When all are cut out, hold a wooden spoon upright over the middle of each cookie; press bowl end of the spoon down all the way to expose baking sheet, then rock it from side to side. This will "part the lips."

Bake in 375 degree oven for 8 minutes. Immediately, before removing cookies from sheet, pinch the corners of the lips up into a smile. Remove carefully from sheet using a spatula and let cookies cool on a rack.

When completely cool, the lips may be painted with a light glaze of egg white and then sprinkled with store-bought red sugar. Depending on the size of the heart cutter used, this recipe makes about 2 dozen cookies.

The Lady's Navel

These voluptuous cookies are made of a tender dough using cream cheese and butter. They get their name because of the depression in the middle—to be left unfilled unless with a flawless diamond.

5 tablespoons butter
⅓ cup sugar
3 ounces cream cheese
1 egg yolk
Grated rind of half a lemon
½ teaspoon baking powder
1⅓ cups flour

All ingredients must be at room temperature. Cream the butter, then beat in the sugar and the cream cheese. Blend in egg yolk and lemon rind. Sift baking powder and flour into the mixture and blend well. Shape the dough between sheets of plastic wrap into several flat rectangles. Chill for an hour. With a rolling pin roll dough between plastic wrap to ¼ inch thickness.

Cut into circles with a 1½- to 2-inch round cookie cutter. The lid from a spice jar works well as a cookie cutter. Place on ungreased baking sheet. With the rounded end of a chopstick or a clean pencil eraser press an indentation into the middle of each cookie.

Bake in 375 degree oven for 15 minutes or until cookies are just beginning to brown. Remove to rack to cool. Makes about 50 cookies.

IV

High Tea

Rarebit
Cornish Pasties
Sally Lunn
Seedcake
Hot Cross Buns
Rum Nicky
Jumbles

High tea is a workingman's supper, a family meal served early in the evening. There is widespread misconception that high tea means formal tea. Unlike high fashion or high church, high tea has nothing to do with starch and propriety. Perhaps on a brisk Sunday afternoon after leaf raking or snow shoveling, or on a Saturday after the football game, high tea has the charm of easy hospitality.

For the convenience and pleasure of the cook who is also the hostess, all the foods are set on the table right at the beginning of the meal. Freshly baked bread warm from the oven—Sally Lunn is a favorite loaf that will fill the house with a good yeasty fragrance. There will be Rarebit, a hot savory dish, or Cornish Pasties and all the sweeter baked goods the table and the appetites can handle. Give the guests and the family a taste of the old traditional favorites—Seedcake, Hot Cross Buns and Rum Nicky.

Three curious oddities of the typical high tea menu must be noted, if not served. Celery, by the stalk, crisp and standing in a cut glass vase with salt available for dipping. And toast served topped with canned baked beans or canned spaghetti.

A notable tea is wanted to fill the teapot. Oolong, from Taiwan, is one of the teas that lies between the green and the black. It is a gentle tea with a fruity flavor often likened to the taste of ripe peaches. It is called the champagne of teas and should be taken "neat"—without milk.

Rarebit

Half the world calls this savory dish of Cheddar cheese melted with beer and served over toast, Rarebit, the other half refers to it as Rabbit. There is as much rabbit in Rabbit as there is woodcock in Scotch Woodcock. It may be prepared ahead of time and reheated on the stove, poured over toast points and then bubbled under the broiler just before serving. More fun, however, since it is simplicity itself to make, is to prepare the Rarebit at the tea table in a chafing dish.

2 tablespoons butter
1 pound Cheddar cheese, grated (about 6 cups)
2 tablespoons cornstarch
1 teaspoon prepared mustard
2 teaspoons Worcestershire sauce
1 cup beer or ale

12 slices bread, toasted and buttered, cut into triangles
Black pepper, freshly ground

In a saucepan over gentle heat, or in the top of a chafing dish over simmering water, melt butter. Toss the grated cheese with the cornstarch and add, stirring constantly. As cheese melts, add mustard, Worcestershire sauce and beer, stirring constantly until smooth and thick.

Spoon over hot buttered toast triangles. Grind black pepper on top with a generous twist of the wrist. Serves 8.

Cornish Pasties

Pronounced "pass-tees," these are the beloved meat pies carried to work by Cornwallian miners. The half-round shape lets them fit handily into a back pocket. They were more familiarly known as Tiddy Oggies, when made with potatoes, or Hoggans, when times were good and meat plentiful enough to leave out the potatoes. But the ongoing question is, "To turnip, or not to turnip." This recipe includes turnips—in token quantity, true— but the cook's conscience may be the guide. All ingredients go into the pasty uncooked, giving a unique flavor, especially from the onions. This also prevents the pasty from being dry as the ingredients "give up" juices during baking.

Pasty Pastry

½ cup butter
½ cup lard
4 cups flour
½ teaspoon salt
8 to 10 tablespoons cold water

Cut both fats into flour until the mixture is coarse and mealy. Add salt. Sprinkle on as much of the cold water as is needed to form a firm dough. Knead lightly into a ball. Refrigerate for at least 1 hour before using.

Pasty Filling

1 large baking potato
1 large carrot
1 small white turnip (or ½ cup diced rutabaga)
1 medium onion, finely chopped
½ teaspoon salt
¼ teaspoon black peppr, freshly ground
1 cup chuck steak (about ½ pound), uncooked, cut into ¼-inch cubes
1 egg, beaten

Peel potato, carrot and turnip and dice them all into ¼-inch cubes. Toss with chopped onion, salt, pepper and meat until well mixed.

Roll out pastry into 5-inch circles. Place about a half cupful of filling on half of each circle. Moisten the edge of this half of the pastry with water, then fold top over to form a half-moon shape. The edges must be firmly sealed using the "Cornish crimp." This "buttoning up" is accomplished by pinching the edges at regular intervals to give a fluted effect.

Place pasties on 2 ungreased baking sheets. Brush each pasty lightly with egg beaten with a few drops of water. Bake at 425 degrees for 10 minutes. Reduce heat to 350 degrees and bake 25 minutes longer. This recipe will make 16 small turnovers or 8 large ones.

Sally Lunn

Each time a recipe for Sally Lunn appears the question is raised: Was there a Miss Sally Lunn or is the name derived from the French words for sun and moon, Sol y Lune? Truly, the only thing that needs to be raised is the dough for this delectable, light tea loaf.

2 packages dry yeast
¼ cup sugar
½ cup warm water (115 degrees)
¾ cup milk, heated
½ cup butter
3 eggs, beaten
1 teaspoon salt
3¾ cups flour

Dissolve yeast with sugar in warm water in a small bowl. Pour hot milk into a large bowl, then add butter cut in pieces. Stir until butter melts. Cool to lukewarm.

Add the yeast mixture and the eggs. Add the salt and half the flour and beat with wooden spoon or electric mixer. Add remaining flour and mix to a smooth, soft batter.

Place in a bowl and cover with a damp cloth. Let dough rise in warm spot until doubled in size—about 1 hour. Beat down with wooden spoon and transfer the dough to a well-buttered Turk's Head mold or a 9-inch tube pan. Cover with damp cloth and place in warm place until again doubled in size—about 30 minutes. Bake in 350 degree oven for 45 to 50 minutes. Serve warm, if possible.

Seedcake

Seedcake is a traditional accompaniment to teatime. Biting into the sharp-flavored caraway seed is not to everyone's taste, so high tech moves in. With a processor or blender or an electric coffee grinder, the caraway seeds are pulverized, and then sifted through a fine strainer. The result is a ground spice in the nutmeg or clove class—but with its own distinctive flavor. The sifted-off unground seeds may be used in rye bread. The ground caraway gives the cake a tawny tint and an intriguing flavor.

> 1 cup butter
> 1 cup sugar
> 3 eggs
> 2 cups flour
> 1 teaspoon baking powder
> 1 teaspoon ground caraway (see above)

Generously butter the bottom and sides of a deep 8-inch round cake pan (a small spring form works well). In a large bowl, cream butter and sugar together until light and fluffy. Add eggs, one at a time, blending well after each.

Sift together flour, baking powder and caraway. Sift again. Add the flour mixture gradually to the creamed mixture. When the batter is well blended, spread it in the prepared pan, smoothing the top with a spatula. Batter will be thick.

Bake in the middle of a 350 degree oven for 50 minutes or until cake begins to pull away from the sides of the pan.

Let the cake cool in the pan for five minutes before turning it out on a rack.

A beautiful finish for seedcake is confectionery sugar sifted over a paper doily. Place the cooled cake on a large sheet of waxed paper. Position and firmly press doily onto the top of the cake. Sift sugar onto it until the doily is completely covered in sugar. Carefully lift doily off and remove cake, preferably to footed cakestand. Remaining sugar on doily goes back into box.

Hot Cross Buns

Although these fruited yeast buns are baked year round it is only during Lent that they are marked with a cross. Long ago one bun was kept from the Good Friday baking and hung from the kitchen rafters for the year.

> 1 package dry yeast
> ¼ cup warm water (115 degrees)
> 1 tablespoon brown sugar
> ⅔ cup milk, scalded
> 2 tablespoons butter
> 2 tablespoons granulated sugar
> ½ teaspoon salt
> 1 egg
> 2 cups flour
> ¼ teaspoon cinnamon
> ¼ teaspoon nutmeg
> ¼ teaspoon allspice
> ¼ cup mixed glacé peel
> ¼ cup currants

Dissolve yeast in water with brown sugar. Meanwhile, scald milk in small saucepan. Remove from heat, cut in butter and stir to melt. Add granulated sugar and salt. In a large bowl, beat egg well and add the milk and yeast mixtures to it.

Sift flour and spices together. Toss peels and currants into it, separating pieces. Add to yeast mixture in large bowl. Beat hard with a wooden spoon for 3 minutes. If necessary, add more flour to make a medium firm dough.

Cover bowl with towel and set over a pan of warm water to rise. Let rise for one hour or until doubled in size. Punch down and cut dough into 16 pieces. Reserve one for crisscross trim. Form the 15 pieces into balls and set them in a well-buttered 9-by 5-inch baking pan. Arrange them in 3 rows across, 5 down. Allow enough space for rolls to expand while rising and baking.

Roll out reserved dough into long, flat strip. With pizza cutter or knife, cut into ⅛-inch strips. Remove pieces of peel and currants that may be on surface of dough. Depending on length of strip, it may be draped across length of pan and sliced between buns with knife, or each bun may be "crossed" individually. Cover and let buns rise again for 15 to 30 minutes.

Bake in 325 degree oven for 15 to 20 minutes or until nicely browned. Glaze tops as soon as they come out of oven. Makes 15 small buns.

Glaze
2 tablespoons confectionery sugar
2 teaspoons milk

Mix into a smooth paste and spread all over buns using a pastry brush.

Rum Nicky

This is a type of tart, traditionally baked on a plate rather than in a deeper pie pan. Its filling—dates and candied ginger and golden raisins spiked with rum—makes it a most unusual kind of pie, at least to our American cousins. A dollop of whipped cream on top of each serving is extremely compatible.

½ cup orange juice
1 cup yellow raisins
2 cups dates, pitted (or 8 ounces)
¼ cup candied ginger slices
1 tablespoon sugar
2 tablespoons rum
1 sheet of puff pastry, thawed (puff pastry is
    available in grocery store freezer cases)
1 egg, beaten

Heat orange juice in small pan to boiling. Add raisins, remove from heat, stir and let sit while raisins plump.

Halve dates and chop ginger. Toss to combine. Stir sugar and rum into raisins and juice.

Roll puff pastry slightly to enlarge it. Place it on an ovenproof dinner plate. Spread dates and ginger on pastry. Stir the beaten egg into the juice mixture and spread it evenly over the dates. Fold the four corners of the pastry up over the filling and pinch the points together. Bake in 350 degree oven for 45 minutes or until nicely browned. Cut in wedges and serve directly from the plate. Makes 8 to 10 servings.

Jumbles

There is nothing dainty about these cookies. They are genuine fist-fillers. Jumbles were so popular at the turn of the century—the 20th—that recipes for them circulated as quickly as good gossip.

2 eggs
⅔ cup sugar
Grated rind of ½ orange
½ cup butter, softened
2 cups flour
¼ teaspoon salt
1 tablespoon baking powder
Granulated or brown sugar

With a mixer, beat eggs until light. Add sugar and orange rind and beat until fluffy. Blend in softened butter.

Sift flour, salt and baking powder all together into the first mixture and blend well.

Drop by heaping tablespoonfuls onto lightly greased baking sheets. Leave ample room between cookies. There will be about 1½ dozen.

Bake in 375 degree oven for 8 to 10 minutes. Immediately after taking cookies from oven, sprinkle tops with granulated or brown sugar and let them cool on a rack.

V

Nursery Tea

Graham Crackers
Chocolate Soup
Tomato Sandwiches
Beef Tea
Pumpkin Buns
Bread and Butter Pudding
Brown Sugar Bears
Zebra Cake

Nursery tea recalls a cast of storybook characters familiar and beloved. Paddington Bear, at teatime, was partial to cream and jam cakes. When Mary Poppins presided at tea, laughter sometimes caused the table, chairs and occupants to rise to the ceiling. But perhaps the most fabled was the Mad Tea Party which Alice attended where the sleeping Dormouse served as a cushion and the Mad Hatter, to get his watch ticking, dunked it into his tea.

Nursery tea requires neither nursery nor tea. The kitchen table on a rainy afternoon or a card table set out-of-doors on a summer day are equally suitable settings. Depending on the season and the temperature, the teapot may properly be filled with lemonade or fruit juice. Cambric tea—shades of Kate Greenaway—is hot milk with as few drops of tea as needed to give it a honey color. Nanny's favorite to make pink cheeks and ward off colds was Beef Tea. Essential is at least one child, dolls and teddy bears and cooperative cats are accustomed to filling out the guest list.

A small play set of cups, saucers and teapot is high priority. Even though miniatures need refilling every second minute, mastering the art of "pouring" is a joy for any child. In a pinch, any small pitcher or creamer will serve. The following recipes make up a grand menu for a very happy unbirthday party. Of course nursery tea will spoil a child's appetite for supper, but, scheduled late in the afternoon of a special occasion, it can serve as the last meal of the day. These recipes use especially wholesome, nutritious ingredients.

But an elaborate spread is not needed. Just a plateful of cookies or more simply the most traditional food of nursery tea—bread and butter—will satisfy. To Toad, of *Wind in the Willows*, being served tea with "a plate piled up with very hot buttered toast, cut thick, very brown on both sides, with the butter running through the holes in it in great golden drops, like honey from the honeycomb, the smell of it simply talked to Toad, with no uncertain voice of warm kitchens, of breakfasts on bright frosty mornings, of cosy parlour firesides on winter evenings when one's ramble was over and slippered feet were propped on the fender; of the purring of contented cats, and the twitter of sleepy canaries."

Graham Crackers

For every city child who never saw a cow there must be a grownup who never considered that Graham Crackers can be baked at home. If only once in a lifetime, every cook ought to make a batch of good old-fashioned Graham Crackers. They're easy to make, crunchy and wholesome. For extra nutrition, replace a spoonful or two of the flour with wheat germ.

2 cups whole wheat pastry flour
½ cup unprocessed bran
   (The above ingredients are found in health food stores. If available, graham flour may be used instead of the wheat pastry flour and bran combination.)
½ cup light brown sugar
⅛ teaspoon salt
1 teaspoon baking powder
½ teaspoon cinnamon
½ cup vegetable oil
⅓ cup milk

Stir all dry ingredients together in a bowl until they are well blended. Add oil and milk. Knead in bowl with hands until liquid is completely absorbed. Butter a baking sheet no smaller than 12 by 15 inches. The crackers are rolled and cut directly on the baking sheet.

Press dough smoothly out with hands, then continue with a rolling pin, rolling the dough right out to the edges of the sheet. With a long spatula or knife, cut into approximately 2-inch squares. Roll a fluted pastry wheel over cuts for decorative crimped edges. With a fork, prick holes in crackers to make them look "store-bought."

Bake in 350 degree oven for 15 minutes. When cool, store airtight. The flavor improves after a day or two of aging. Makes at least 2½ dozen.

Chocolate Soup

Chocolate Soup is properly served in a cup on a saucer with a soup spoon. A homemade Graham Cracker resting on the saucer is a perfect accompaniment.

> ½ cup milk
> ¼ cup cream or evaporated milk
> 2 teaspoons sugar
> ½ teaspoon vanilla
> 1 heaping teaspoon cocoa
> 1 egg yolk

Heat milk and cream or evaporated milk. Pour from pan into cup leaving about 2 teaspoonsful in pan. Add sugar, vanilla and cocoa to milk in pan and mix to a smooth paste. Add egg yolk and stir over low to medium heat. Gradually stir in heated milk. Stir until blended and thick. This makes one serving—increase quantities to make larger amounts at one time.

Tomato Sandwiches

Although tomatoes, mayonnaise and bread individually are not uncommon foods to children, they become a novelty when combined into a tea sandwich. Notice that the directions call for bread crusts to be cut from bread. These sandwiches will *not* be successful if crusts are left on and furthermore will in no way weaken children's teeth or character. (Conscience may be salved by turning the crusts into bread crumbs for other use.)

> 8 slices bread
> Mayonnaise
> 2 tomatoes
> Salt and pepper

Roll each slice of bread with a rolling pin. (Compare the size of the bread before and after rolling—instant stretching of the food budget!) Spread with mayonnaise.

Slice tomatoes through horizontally in very thin slices. If the sandwiches are to be made up ahead of time and if the tomatoes are especially juicy, squeeze them out lightly while slicing so that bread will not get soggy. Overlap the tomato slices on bread. Salt and pepper them and put on top slices of bread. Trim crusts off and cut into bite-sized segments. Cut one into 4 fingers, another into triangles, another into squares. Makes 16 small sandwiches.

Beef Tea

This is the recipe for the real thing. Bouillon cubes may be used instead to make instant Beef Tea by the cupful.

> 1 pound of chuck or round steak, finely ground
> 3 cups cold water
> 1 teaspoon salt
> 4 peppercorns
> 1 carrot, pared

Place the meat in the top of a double boiler along with the water, salt, peppercorns and carrot. Bring the water in the bottom of the boiler to a boil slowly and let liquid in the top pot simmer for one hour. Cool, then strain. Store in refrigerator until serving time. Serve hot. Makes 3 cups.

Pumpkin Buns

Blessings on the plump golden Pumpkin Bun. Baked with a shiny copper penny in the center—for children old enough not to swallow it—these buns are never-to-be-forgotten nursery food.

¾ cup milk, scalded
¼ cup butter
1 cup pumpkin purée
1½ teaspoons salt
Grated rind from ½ orange
1 package dry yeast
⅓ cup light brown sugar
¼ cup warm water (115 degrees)
3½ cups white flour
1 cup whole wheat flour

Pour the hot milk into a large bowl. Cut butter in and stir until it melts. Add pumpkin, salt and grated orange rind and stir until well blended.

Stir yeast and brown sugar into warm water until dissolved. Add this mixture to the pumpkin mixture and combine well.

Add half of the white flour and beat until batter is smooth. Add whole wheat flour and enough of the remaining white flour to make a soft dough. Place remaining flour on board, add the dough, and knead until smooth and stretchy. Place in greased bowl and turn the dough to coat it evenly. Cover bowl with waxed paper and then with a towel and set in a warm place to rise until doubled in size (about 1½ hours).

Punch down dough and knead briefly into a long log shape. With a knife slice lengthwise in half. Cut through both strips to make a total of 24 pieces. Flatten each piece, knead 4 sides into center—encasing a penny, if desired—pinch together and smooth into a round ball. Place each, pinched side down, in muffin tins or space on greased baking sheets. Cover and let rise until doubled again (about 45 minutes). Bake in 350 degree oven for 20 minutes or until buns take on a golden color. Makes 24 buns.

Bread and Butter Pudding

This is classic nursery food. Despite or perhaps because of its innocent ingredients, bread and butter pudding turns up frequently as the dessert at the end of a very sophisticated dinner. It is said to have been the favorite dessert of the Duchess of Windsor. Sometimes it is gussied up with raisins, candied fruit, cream and the like, but this recipe goes back to basics—with delightful results.

It is, of course, a good way to use up stale bread. White bread makes a finer, delicate pudding, but whole grain bread may be used, too.

Butter
8 slices white bread
4 eggs
3 cups milk
½ cup sugar
1 teaspoon vanilla
Confectionery sugar

Generously butter the bottom and sides of a casserole-type pie dish. Place one slice of bread in center. Cut 3 slices in half crosswise and fit 5 of these into dish around center slice. Cut remaining half slice into triangles to fill in any gaps. (An 8-inch square baking pan may be used instead. Fit 4 slices in bottom of pan, trimming to fit.) Butter the remaining 4 slices generously on one side. Place them buttered side up over the first layer of bread.

Break 4 eggs into a medium-sized bowl. Whisk them a few minutes, then add milk, sugar and vanilla and mix all together. Pour over bread in baking dish. Let sit for ½ hour.

Set baking dish in a larger pan filled with hot, but not boiling, water and slide into 325 degree oven. Bake for 45 minutes or until knife inserted in center comes out dry. Just before serving sprinkle confectionery sugar over top. Serve warm from baking dish. Makes 6 to 8 servings.

Brown Sugar Bears

These cookie beasts are made with rye flour to give them a nutty flavor and extra nutrition, with enough leavening to make them plump, and are dusted with a mixture of cocoa and confectionery sugar to give them a nice woolly coat. If a bear-shaped cookie cutter is not available, see directions at end of recipe for assembling bears from cut-out circles—a fine job for the children.

½ cup butter
½ cup brown sugar
2 eggs
1 tablespoon vanilla
1 cup rye flour
2 cups white flour
2 teaspoons baking powder
1 tablespoon cocoa
Black currants, confectionery sugar, cocoa

Cream butter. Add sugar. Beat in one egg and then the other. Mix in vanilla. Stir together both flours, baking powder and 1 tablespoon cocoa.

Combine the two mixtures and knead until well blended. Refrigerate for several hours or overnight.

Roll dough to ¼-inch thickness—or more, depending on how fat a bear is desired. To make bears without a cutter use round cookie cutters or the rims of drinking glasses, bottle tops, jar lids, etc. Cut 1 large circle for bear's body, a slightly smaller one for the head, 4 smaller circles for paws and a fifth small circle cut in half for ears. Press the circles together, overlapping slightly. Add 2 black currants for eyes, another one for nose.

Bake on greased cookie sheet in 350 degree oven for 10 minutes or until edges just begin to brown. Remove to wax paper. Mix together 1 tablespoon cocoa and 2 tablespoons confectionery sugar. Sift over cookies from shaker or through strainer until bears have a good warm coat. The number of Brown Sugar Bears that this recipe makes varies greatly depending on their size but it is a constant that it never makes enough.

Zebra Cake

Zebra cake by any other name would never taste as good. Those who would insist on calling it marble cake have no imagination.

> ½ cup butter
> 1 cup sugar
> 2 cups cake flour
> 1 tablespoon baking powder
> ¾ cup milk
> 2 tablespoons cocoa
> 1 tablespoon molasses
> 3 egg whites

Cream butter, add sugar gradually and beat until fluffy.

Sift flour with baking powder. Add alternately with the milk to butter mixture. Beat until smooth. Remove 1 cup of batter and place in small mixing bowl. Blend cocoa and molasses into it.

Beat egg whites until they hold a peak. Fold them gently into white cake batter.

Grease 9 × 5-inch loaf pan. Spoon white batter and dark batter alternately into pan in long stripes. Run a knife through batter lengthwise so that when cake is cut, each slice will have a zebra stripe pattern.

Bake in 350 degree oven for 45 minutes or until cake tester inserted in center comes out dry. Makes 16 slices.

VI

A Russian Easter Tea

Farina Pudding

Kulich

Pashka

Kisel

Pour Kisel, Spoon Kisel

Mazurkas

Charlotka

Black Bread

Caramel Color

Meringue Mushrooms

Candied Fruits

Cranberries, Pears

The steaming samovar is the crown of the Russian tea table. Besides boiling water, it provides a hot place to rest the china teapot containing the dark, strong brew. The samovar's elaborate ornamentation—brass, silver, gold or combinations of all—

invites the guests' contemplation as an objet d'art and at the same
time establishes the owner's prosperity. But perhaps most of all,
the samovar radiates both a real and a symbolic warmth to the
guests.

Around the table, the guests gather for toasts and tears,
jokes, songs and stories, gossip and blessings. Russians, it has
been said, discuss their souls as others discuss the weather. At
least one poet must be included in the guest list.

At Easter, eggs, a symbol of eternal life, are an important
part of the celebration. Almost as reliably as a favorite laying hen
produced for the farmer's wife, the jeweler Fabergé created
jeweled eggs for the Czar to give as Easter trinkets. Glorious
baubles they were, trimmed in gold, precious jewels and pearls.
And with the same love of ornamentation, the peasants turned
their eggs into works of art—dyed in deep jewel colors, orange
from onion skins, blue from red cabbage, red from beets, or
painted in patterns as intricate as a Byzantine mosaic.

And eggs, in abundance, go into the Easter holiday food—
especially into the beloved Pashka and Kulich. The Kulich, a
fragrant, rich yeast cake, is baked in a tall cylindrical shape, its
top covered with a sugar icing coaxed to drip generously down
the sides. A tall candle is set into its top and roses—of sugar,
paper or real—are entwined about the candle. Traditionally taken
to mass to be blessed by the priest, back home the Kulich is sliced
and spread with the creamy Pashka.

When the Czar entertained it was not unusual for a hundred
different dishes to be set out. The recipes here are fewer in
number but royal in flavor. There is Charlotka, a molded apple
pudding that gleams with an apricot glaze. There are recipes for
Kisel, the jewel-colored fruit dessert to serve by itself or with
Farina Pudding. There are Mazurkas, Easter cakes made with
hazelnuts and honey. Meringue Mushrooms—here it's a toss-up
whether the greater pleasure lies in the making or in the eating.
And to sweeten the tea—breathtakingly beautiful candied fruits
prepared in a simple, foolproof way.

Russian Caravan is a tea blend that might be served. Blended to the taste of the Czarist Russian society, it is usually a combination of Keemun, Assam and China Green—well suited to anyone's samovar. It is also marketed under the names Russian Blossom and Russian Style. If possible, the tea is served in glass cups with silver handles. On a very bitterly cold day, tea is served with a jigger of rum and a slice of lemon stuck with a clove.

To turn the Russian Easter tea into a more exuberant meal, follow the recipe for a loaf of good hearty Black Bread and add platters of brightly dyed and decorated boiled eggs, sliced ham, herring, smoked salmon, caviar and iced vodka.

Farina Pudding

This pudding is a lot like Clark Kent—mild tempered and very attractive. A very Old World pudding. The farina mixture, when chilled, gels beautifully into a showy, snowy mold. Topped with Kisel it is a lovely sight.

> ½ cup farina
> 1 cup boiling water
> 1 cup milk
> ⅓ cup sugar
> 1 teaspoon vanilla
> 2 egg whites

Add farina all at once to boiling water in saucepan and stir vigorously with a wooden spoon until smooth. Continue to stir while adding milk and sugar. When mixture bubbles, lower heat and continue to stir. Mixture will be very thick. Remove from heat and stir in vanilla. Beat egg whites until stiff and fold into farina mixture. Pour into fancy mold rinsed in cold water. Refrigerate overnight or until very cold. Just before serving turn out onto shallow plate. Makes 6 servings.

Kulich

Traditionally a tall round loaf, it has even been baked in stovepipes—but a large juice or coffee can works fine. Often the dough rises above the can making a loaf reminiscent of a mushroom or an onion-domed Byzantine tower. To serve, cut off the cap, slice the Kulich crosswise and serve in rounds or half-rounds. The near-necessary accompaniment to Kulich is the creamy fruit and nut studded spread called Pashka.

¾ cup milk
½ teaspoon sugar
1 package dry yeast
½ cup confectionery sugar
3 cups flour
3 eggs yolks, beaten
1 teaspoon vanilla
½ cup butter, softened
¼ cup candied fruit and peel
¼ cup yellow raisins
¼ cup almonds, blanched and chopped

Prepare a pan by buttering the inside of a large juice can (7 inches tall) or a 2-pound coffee can. Heat milk to 115 degrees and add sugar. Sprinkle yeast over milk and let soften for a few minutes, then stir. Sift confectionery sugar and flour into large mixing bowl. Add egg yolks, vanilla and yeast mixture and stir. Cut butter into small pieces and knead it into dough with hands. Continue gently kneading dough in bowl or on lightly floured board for about 10 minutes or until dough has become smooth and stretchy.

Turn dough in a buttered bowl to coat, cover with cloth and place in warm spot to rise.

Spin candied fruit and peel in blender or processor briefly to reduce size of pieces. This step is not necessary but adds both to appearance and taste by distributing the wealth of the fruit more evenly.

Combine raisins, candied fruit and almonds.

When dough has about doubled in size, punch down. On board dusted lightly with flour, knead dough gently while incorporating handfuls of the fruit and nuts mixture. Knead just until all are distributed throughout. Form into a smooth ball and slide down into prepared can. Heat oven to 350 degrees after removing all but one shelf placed in bottom rack. Let dough rise again in warm spot for 10 minutes or until dough reaches close to top of pan. Place in center of oven and bake for 35 to 40 minutes. Allow to cool in can for 15 minutes. If removal is difficult, turn upside down and run bottom through can opener. Using can bottom, push loaf out through top.

Frost while still warm with a thin white glaze.

Icing

½ cup confectionery sugar
1 tablespoon cold water
2 teaspoons fresh lemon juice, strained

Mix together sugar, water and lemon juice until smooth. Spread glaze on top of Kulich, letting it drip down the sides. When serving, a lit candle is often placed in the center.

Pashka

This creamy delicacy served as a genuine Easter celebration dish combines many of the foods given up for the old Orthodox Lenten fast—eggs, butter, cream and cheese. It is formed, traditionally, in a flattened pyramidal mold made of wood with the imprint XB carved into the side, meaning Christ is Risen. In America, Pashka is invariably made in a clay flower pot. The cone shape resembles somewhat the original and the clay, like the wood, allows the liquid from the ingredients to drain away so that it may be successfully unmolded. A better choice may be a pint-sized wooden berry box. Its shape, though shorter, is quite authentic. Preparing Pashka is a good way to use some of the egg yolks separated from their whites in the making of Meringue Mushrooms described on page 68. Pashka must be made at least one day ahead of time and two or three days are better.

    1 pound pot cheese (or cottage cheese)
    ½ cup butter, softened
    1 cup sour cream
    8 ounces cream cheese
    3 egg yolks
    ½ cup sugar
    ½ cup candied fruit, chopped
    2 tablespoons candied peel, chopped
    1 teaspoon vanilla
    ¼ cup almonds, blanched and finely chopped

Prepare flower pot. It must be scrubbed well inside and out and then set in a warm oven or in the hot sun to dry thoroughly.

Place the pot cheese in a double layer of cheese cloth in a colander. Place a heavy weight on the top and let it drain for three hours.

Force cheese through a fine sieve. Add the butter, sour cream, cream cheese and mix well.

In a separate bowl beat egg yolks and sugar with a whisk or electric mixture until light colored and thick. Combine with cheese mixture. Transfer to a saucepan and cook over very low heat, stirring constantly, until it thickens. Do not boil. Remove from heat and stir in fruit, peel and vanilla. Immediately set pan in a bowl of ice water to cool it quickly. Stir in almonds when it is cool. Line the berry box or the prepared flower pot with a double layer of cheese cloth. When cheese mixture has begun to thicken transfer it to mold. Cover with a cloth napkin and set a weight on top. Place mold over small bowl or large cup so that it will be raised above the liquid that will drain from it. Refrigerate overnight.

To serve, turn out onto plate. Carefully remove cheesecloth. Pashka may be trimmed with bits of candied fruit. Makes about 12 servings.

Kisel

Kisel is a smooth, slippery dessert made from any one of many different fruits—strawberry, plum, cranberry, orange. When made from juice it is thickened to pouring consistency. Pour Kisel is most often used as a topping for a popular pudding made with farina (see recipe, p.57). When puréed fruit is used the Kisel is thickened to become a spoon dessert. When a thickener such as arrowroot is used, the result is a shining jewel-like color. Arrowroot gives the most delicate results, but potato starch or cornstarch may be used instead. Kisel is a year-round favorite made from preserved fruit as well as fresh. So simple to make, it is a refreshing change from artificially flavored commercial gelatin desserts.

Pour Kisel

Orange Juice
1¾ cups orange juice, strained
1 tablespoon sugar
1 tablespoon plus 1 teaspoon arrowroot

Cranberry Juice
1¾ cups bottled cranberry juice
1 tablespoon plus 1 teaspoon arrowroot

Heat all but ¼ cup of the juice in a saucepan. Add sugar to orange juice (cranberry juice is already sweet enough). Meanwhile, dissolve arrowroot in reserved cold juice. When juice boils, add the thickener mixture. Bring to a boil again, stirring all the while, until mixture turns from milky to transparent. Remove from heat and cool several hours before serving. Kisel thickens as it cools.

Spoon Kisel

Apple Kisel

>2 pounds apples, peeled and cored
>3 cups water
>½ cup sugar
>1 tablespoon plus 1 teaspoon arrowroot
>2 tablespoons water

Cranberry Kisel

>4 cups fresh cranberries (12-ounce package)
>2½ cups water
>¾ cup sugar
>1 tablespoon plus 1 teaspoon arrowroot
>2 tablespoons water

Put the fruit and water in a saucepan and bring to a boil. Reduce heat and simmer 15 minutes or until fruit is soft. Press fruit through a sieve into a bowl. Return to saucepan, add sugar and bring quickly to a boil. Reduce heat to medium and stir in the arrowroot dissolved in 2 tablespoons water. Stir constantly until fruit boils, turns transparent and thickens slightly. Chill well before serving.

Instead of straining fruit it may be spun in a blender, which will make Kisel more fruity but with a coarser texture.

Mazurkas

Little cakes made of honey and beaten eggs, with finely ground nuts to take the place of flour. Hazelnuts, also called Filberts, are authentic but other nuts may substitute. Mazurkas are a sweet, puffy confection. As no amount of generous buttering of the pan will prevent them from sticking, they must be baked in paper cups. Small white nut cups are a perfect size for one wonderful mouthful.

> 3 eggs, separated
> ½ cup honey
> 1 tablespoon grated lemon rind from one large lemon
> 1 tablespoon fresh lemon juice
> 1½ cups hazelnuts ground
> 1 tablespoon sugar
> Whipped cream

With an electric mixer or whisk, beat egg yolks until they lighten to a lemon color. While continuing to beat slowly, add honey. Beat until the mixture forms a feather pattern in the batter. Beat in the grated lemon rind and juice. Fold in the nuts.

With clean beaters beat egg whites until frothy. Gradually add sugar and beat until stiff peaks form. Gently combine the two mixtures. Spoon the batter into paper cups set on baking sheet and bake in the center of a 350 degree oven for 15 to 20 minutes or until lightly browned. Turn off oven heat and let the Mazurkas sit in the oven with the door open for 10 minutes.

Just before serving, each Mazurka may be topped with a dollop of stiffly beaten whipped cream dusted with a sprinkle of nutmeg. Makes about 24.

Charlotka

While the Czar was in the palace eating his favorite Charlotte Russe, the people were enjoying their charlotte—a different, simpler affair made with apples—but equally delicious. A loaf of bread, a splash of wine and thou can easily put together this beautiful creation.

> Bread (white, home-style, as thinly sliced as possible,
>   about 10 slices depending on the size of mold used)
> Butter (up to ¼ cup)
> 8 to 10 apples of a tart variety
> ½ cup sugar
> Juice and grated rind of ½ lemon
> ¼ cup white wine
> 4 ounces apricot preserves
> 1 tablespoon brandy or apricot liqueur

Generously butter one side of enough slices of bread to completely line the bottom and sides of a mold. (Any deep, round ovenproof bowl will do as well as a proper charlotte mold.) Cut off crusts. (Crusts may be turned into crumbs and mixed into apple mixture.) Cut two slices diagonally in half to form triangles. Place these four triangles in bottom center of mold with points meeting in center. Fill out from this, cutting and fitting so that bread completely covers the inside of the bowl. Bread need not overlap but must meet closely. If pieces extend above top of bowl, do not cut them as they will be folded down later.

Peel, quarter and core apples. Grate, blend or process apples coarsely and combine with sugar, lemon juice, grated rind and wine. Fill bread-lined mold with apple mixture. Completely cover top of mold with more buttered bread slices, buttered side up.

Bake in 350 degree oven for 45 minutes. Cool in mold for 15 minutes. Invert mold onto serving dish and allow to set 10 minutes more before removing mold. Meanwhile, heat apricot preserves, stirring in 1 tablespoon of water to thin. When preserves are syrupy, remove from heat and strain through sieve. Stir in brandy. Remove mold from Charlotka and spoon apricot syrup over to glaze completely. Serve warm. Makes 8 servings.

Black Bread

A hearty, chewy peasant bread that needs only sweet butter spread on it. Without the addition of caramel color this recipe will produce a *brown*, but still delicious, loaf.

1 cup warm water (115 degrees)
1 package dry yeast
¼ cup vegetable oil
1 tablespoon cocoa
1½ teaspoons instant coffee powder or crystals
3 tablespoons dark molasses
2 tablespoons caramel color, optional (recipe follows)
1 tablespoon vinegar
2 cups flour
1 cup rye flour
1 cup bran
2 tablespoons corn meal
2 teaspoons salt
¼ teaspoon fennel seeds, ground in mortar
Corn meal and bran

Put water in large bowl. Stir in yeast and set aside. Pour oil into measuring cup. Add cocoa and stir into a smooth paste. Add to this the coffee powder, molasses, caramel color and vinegar. Combine with yeast mixture.

Combine flour, rye flour, bran, 2 tablespoons corn meal, salt and ground fennel. Add to yeast mixture and work together with hands. On well-floured board knead 10 minutes or until smooth and stretchy—or a processor can make light work of this heavy dough.

Place in greased bowl, turning ball to coat well. Place bowl over (but not in) pot of warm water and cover with damp towel. Let rise 1½ to 2½ hours or until doubled. Punch down gently and knead into a round ball. Pinch any seams well to prevent unfolding and cracking during rising and baking.

Sprinkle a little corn meal on bottom of an 8-inch cake pan. Place round loaf on it. Sprinkle top with a scant handful of bran and lightly press it in. Cover with damp towel again and let rise until doubled—about 1 hour. Bake in 350 degree oven for 45 minutes or until loaf gives back a hard hollow sound when thumped on bottom. As difficult as it is to resist bread warm from the oven, allowing this loaf to mellow overnight improves the flavor decidedly.

Caramel Color
½ cup sugar
½ cup water

In a heavy skillet mix together sugar and water. Cook over medium high heat, stirring occasionally, but watching constantly, until syrup turns almost black. Additional water may need to be added but add it to the boiling mixture by the dropful to avoid being burned by splattering.

Store in a glass jar at room temperature. The addition of Caramel Color to the ingredients will color but not sweeten the dough.

Meringue Mushrooms

Mushrooms, like eggs, are a food with symbolic ties to mysticism. In Russia, mushroom hunting is a national pastime. Meringue Mushrooms, on the other hand, are food foolery unparalleled. They require a little determination and a dry day. Fun to make, a delectable puff of a mouthful, they also make a dear centerpiece.

> ¾ cup confectionery sugar
> ⅛ teaspoon cream of tartar
> ½ teaspoon vanilla
> 3 egg whites at room temperature
> 2 ounces baking chocolate, sweet or semisweet
> Cocoa

Position oven racks so that cookies will bake in lower half of oven. Preheat oven to 225 degrees. (That's 225 degrees, not 325 degrees!) Cover 2 baking sheets with foil. Place a plain round large tip with ¼ to ½ inch diameter opening into a pastry bag. Turn back cuff on pastry bag and stand it up in a drinking glass—ready to be filled.

Sift sugar to make sure it is lump-free. Measure out cream of tartar, sugar and vanilla and have them standing by before beating egg whites. Beaters and bowl must be absolutely free of grease to get greatest volume from egg whites.

Place egg whites in small, deep bowl and begin beating. Add cream of tartar. When whites hold a peak, add vanilla and begin adding sugar a tablespoonful at a time while beating continuously on high speed. Beat until the whites are very stiff—ten minutes of beating time will be minimum. Remove beaters and transfer meringue mixture to pastry bag.

Stems: Pipe these first to gain practice. They are piped onto baking sheet as upstanding tubes. Bases should be broad, narrowing slightly to the top for realism and to balance the caps. The top of the stem need not be flat as they are easily leveled off after baking with a paring knife. If foil on baking sheet slips, secure it with a few dabs of meringue between foil and sheet. Make about 35 stems (that allows for some failures) widely spaced on sheet. Place them in the oven at once (don't wait for the caps to be formed) and set timer for one hour.

Caps: Pipe a fat round blob for each cap. Keep tip down on sheet and let meringue billow up around it. Ignore peaks of meringue that may form—they will be taken care of later. Make as many caps as stems. When all caps are formed, rub fingertip over an ice cube. With cold fingertip lightly smooth peaks. Place in oven, noting time.

Baking: Meringues are more to be dried than baked. They must not brown or flavor will be affected. They must be dried completely or they will be sticky and perishable. When done they should be crisp to the touch and snap or peel easily off the foil. Leave the stems on the foil for ease in assembling mushrooms.

Finishing: When caps have finished baking, melt chocolate in cup placed in pan of warm water. Dip bottom of each cap in chocolate, coating it evenly, then place it atop a stem. When chocolate has hardened, sift cocoa over caps. With fingertips, lightly smudge cocoa in to give all-over color. Then sift lightly again with cocoa.

Huddle the Meringue Mushrooms together on a plate covered with moss or in wooden berry or mushroom baskets.

Candied Fruits

Beautiful, translucent candied fruit seen in gourmet shops at breathtaking prices can be made simply in the oven. A selection of jewel-like apples, pears or cranberries arranged on a small glass plate gives an elegant touch when served to each guest to sweeten the tea.

Cranberries treated in this manner are a surprise—they look and taste more like tart cherries. As the cherry season is so short and cranberries are available a relatively long time at reasonable prices, they make a wonderful substitute.

Cranberries
½ pound fresh cranberries
½ cup sugar

Rinse and dry the cranberries. Use only perfect, plump ones, the larger the better. Sprinkle half the sugar evenly in a large, shallow pan. Arrange cranberries over the sugar. Try to keep them from touching. Sift the remaining ¼ cup of sugar over them. Cover tightly with lid or aluminum foil. Bake in 350 degree oven for 30 to 45 minutes or until sugar has dissolved and berries are soft and translucent.

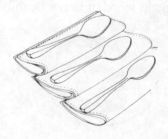

Pears
½ cup sugar
3 ripe pears

Sprinkle half the sugar evenly in a large, shallow pan. Remove stems and peel pears. Slice horizontally through the pear, making circles about ⅛-inch thick. Remove seeds but otherwise leave core intact as it forms a beautiful star design. Lay pear slices on sugar so that they do not touch. Sift remaining ¼ cup of sugar over the pears. Cover with tight-fitting lid or aluminum foil. Bake in 350 degree oven for 30 minutes or until sugar has melted and pears are soft and translucent.

Apples are prepared in the same manner as pears but they should be cut in slices, rather than cut crosswise through the fruit. Use a firm variety.

VII

Tea for Two

White Bread
Whole Wheat Bread
Watercress Sandwiches
Real Cinnamon Toast
Cream Patties
Brandy Snaps
Love Letters
Trilbys
Chocolate Cake

"Tea for Two" was the 18th-century advertising cry of tea for tuppence a pot—a kind of price war against the going rate of thruppence. The present meaning as a cozy tête à tête is much preferred. It conjures up visions of specially-baked sugar cakes and unlisted telephones, of a string quartet playing Haydn on the phonograph. A romantic Valentine's Day rendezvous that doesn't have to occur on February 14th. The recognized soul- and body-warming qualities of tea and its accompanying food are an irresistible foil for an afternoon's lazy flirtation. In Edwardian days a gentleman calling on a lady at teatime left his cane and gloves laid conspicuously across a chair at the door as a Do Not Disturb sign.

Start with Watercress Sandwiches, a veritable teatime prop. Then a plate of disarmingly naive Cinnamon Toast kept warm wrapped in a linen napkin. On a footed dish an offering of best cookies—Brandy Snaps, old-fashioned Trilbys and not-so-subtle Love Letters. Waiting on the side, a very intemperate Chocolate Cake.

With this sweet menu a safe tea to serve is Darjeeling. Grown along the slopes of the Himalayan Mountains, it is one of the world's most prized teas. Some tasters detect in it the subtle flavor of black currant. Darjeeling has a rich golden-red color and an exquisite bouquet that makes it particularly amiable with sweets. Or dare to serve Ginseng—an herbal tea with a pleasant licorice-like taste. It is made from a wild, forked root with a resemblance to the human form. Once literally worth its weight in gold, it is believed to contain the earth's essence in condensed form and so to have medicinal properties. Aphrodisia is said to be among its extraordinary powers.

White Bread

This simple, very basic recipe for one loaf of White Bread is ideal for any of the tea sandwiches described in this book. It will also serve admirably in the preparation of Charlotka, Bread and Butter Pudding, Rarebit and Woodcock.

If baked in a bread pan with a slide-on cover (called pan de mies or pullman) it can not rise above the pan, will have a very fine, close texture and will cut into trim square slices. This recipe is for a loaf pan with a 7- to 8-cup volume. If possible use one with straight, not angled, sides. To improvise a lid place a sheet of foil on top of pan (buttered on the side facing down) and cover with a baking sheet with a weight on it.

To make things simple, start-to-finish directions are given after the ingredients for making the bread both by hand and by processor.

> 1 package yeast
> 1 tablespoon sugar
> ⅓ cup warm water (115 degrees)
> 4 tablespoons butter
> ⅓ cup boiling water
> 1 egg
> 1½ teaspoons salt
> 3 cups unbleached white flour

Hand Mixing

Dissolve yeast and sugar in warm water in a small bowl. Meanwhile, cut butter into small pieces into a large mixing bowl. Pour on ⅓ cup boiling water and stir until butter melts. Beat in egg and salt. (The melting butter should lower the temperature of the water so that it will not cook the egg. If butter is room temperature when added, allow the mixture to cool slightly before adding egg.) With a wooden spoon stir in yeast mixture. Add 1 cup of flour and mix well. Add remaining flour and knead in bowl or on floured board. If dough is sticky, knead in additional flour; if too dry, sprinkle with a few drops of water. Knead until dough becomes smooth and stretchy. Shape into a smooth ball, place in greased bowl and turn to coat all over. Cover with plastic wrap or a damp towel and set to rise in a warm place until dough has doubled in size (1 to 2 hours).

Deflate dough and knead briefly. Form into a ball, return to bowl, turning it again to coat. Cover, place in warm spot until dough doubles from original size (about 45 minutes). This extra rising adds to the fine texture of the loaf.

Deflate dough and pat into a rectangle. Fold in half length-wise, pinch edges together, turn the ends under and place the loaf, seam down, into a greased loaf pan. Cover and let dough rise until pan is ¾ full.

If desired, bake the bread without a lid—it will rise above the pan and have a fat, rounded top. In this case, let the dough rise to the top of the pan before baking.

If using a bread pan without a slide-on cover, place foil (butter side facing dough) and baking sheet on top and weight down with a heavy oven-proof object such as a rock or a brick. Bake in the middle of a 375 degree oven for 35 to 40 minutes. Loaf should sound hollow when thumped. Cool thoroughly on a rack before slicing or wrapping.

Processor Mixing

Dissolve yeast with sugar and warm water in processor bowl fitted with metal blade by spinning for 5 seconds. Scrape down sides of bowl with a rubber spatula, if necessary, and spin again briefly. Cut butter into small pieces into a small bowl. Pour on boiling water and stir until butter melts. Beat in egg and salt. (The melting butter should lower the temperature of the water so that it will not cook the egg. If butter is room temperature when added, allow the mixture to cool slightly before adding egg.)

Add 2 cups of the flour to the yeast mixture and process by turning on and off several times. Add butter mixture and blend with several on-and-off turns. Add the remaining cup of flour in 3 parts, processing after each addition. When dough has formed a ball let it spin on blade for half a minute. If ball does not form, trickle in additional water until it does. If dough is sticky, sprin-kle with 1 or 2 tablespoons additional flour and turn machine on and off several times to coat dough. Remove and knead dough briefly by hand to check that it is smooth and stretchy.

Shape dough into a small ball, place in greased bowl and

turn to coat all over. Cover with plastic wrap or a damp towel and set to rise in a warm place until dough has doubled in size (1 to 2 hours).

Deflate dough and knead briefly. Form into a ball, return to bowl, turning it again to coat. Cover, place in warm spot until dough doubles from original size (about 45 minutes). This extra rising adds to the fine texture of the loaf.

Deflate dough and pat into a rectangle. Fold in half lengthwise, pinch edges together, turn the ends under and place the loaf, seam down, into greased loaf pan. Cover and let dough rise until pan is ¾ full. If desired, bake the bread without a lid—it will rise above the pan and have a fat, rounded top. In this case, let the dough rise to the top of the pan before baking.

If using a bread pan without a slide-on cover, place foil (butter side facing dough) and baking sheet on top and weight down with a heavy oven-proof object such as a rock or a brick. Bake in the middle of a 375 degree oven for 35 to 40 minutes. Loaf should sound hollow when thumped. Cool thoroughly on a rack before slicing or wrapping.

Whole Wheat Bread

Follow the directions for White Bread but make these changes in the ingredients: for the white sugar substitute 1 to 2 tablespoons of brown sugar, honey or molasses; replace half of the unbleached white flour with whole wheat flour.

Watercress Sandwiches

Watercress
6 slices brown bread, thinly sliced
2 tablespoons butter
1 teaspoon lemon juice
Salt

Wash watercress and discard stems, saving a few of the smallest sprigs for garnishing. Pat leaves dry on a towel. Beat the lemon juice and the butter together until smooth. Spread on bread. Trim the crusts.

Arrange enough watercress leaves to make a thin layer on half of the bread slices. Sprinkle lightly with salt. Top with remaining slices. Cut each into four squares. Cover with a damp tea towel and chill. Just before serving tuck small sprigs or leaves here and there between the layers. Makes 12 tea sandwiches.

Real Cinnamon Toast

As opposed to bread run through a toaster and sprinkled with cinnamon and sugar, this method gives an entirely different aspect to a cozy treat. Select a bread with a solid crumb—home-made or home-style bread.

9 slices white bread
⅓ cup butter
½ cup sugar (white sugar or half white, half brown)
1 teaspoon cinnamon

Trim the crusts from the bread and cut each slice into 2 triangles. Melt the butter and use a pastry brush to coat the triangles lightly but thoroughly, top and bottom and all edges as well.

On a saucer, blend the sugar and cinnamon. With fingers, sift sugar over each triangle until completely coated.

Place the triangles on a rack and place the rack on a baking sheet. Bake in center of 350 degree oven for 5 minutes. Switch heat control from bake to broil and watch toast until top bubbles. Toast may be previously prepared to the point before broiling and warmed and broiled just before serving. Makes 18 triangular slices.

Cream Patties

1 cup confectionery sugar
1 tablespoon corn syrup
1 tablespoon butter
1 tablespoon margarine
A pinch of salt
Flavorings
Food colors

Mix all ingredients together until blended. Dust a marble slab or a counter top with additional confectionery sugar and knead until satiny. Divide into four portions.

Flavor and tint each portion to suit fancy. To prevent over-dosing with flavoring extracts, pour a tiny amount into bottle cap and drip drops from this. The liquid from the flavoring and color may make candy sticky—if so, knead in a bit more confectionery sugar. Exposure to air and refrigerator will stiffen the patties.

Suggestions for flavoring:
2 drops cherry or strawberry extract and 1 drop red coloring
1 drop mint extract and 1 drop green coloring
2 drops almond extract and 1 drop yellow coloring
2 teaspoons cocoa

Wrap each portion in plastic. When all are flavored and tinted roll each into logs and cut ½-inch-sized slices. Roll into ball. Flatten with the tines of a fork into flat patty. Store, covered in refrigerator.

Brandy Snaps

The heat of the oven puddles this cookie dough into flat rounds which bake into lacy discs. While still warm from the oven they are rolled around a wooden broom handle or formed into a cornucopia. Bake one first to try out the technique. Just before serving, pipe whipped cream sweetened with sugar and spiked with brandy into the snaps—or fill them with vanilla ice cream.

> 2 tablespoons molasses
> 2 tablespoons corn syrup
> ¼ cup margarine
> ⅓ cup sugar
> ¾ teaspoon ground ginger
> 1 teaspoon grated lemon rind
> ½ cup flour
> 2 teaspoons brandy

In a saucepan heat molasses and corn syrup to boiling. Add margarine and stir until melted. Add sugar, ginger and grated lemon rind and stir until sugar has melted. Remove from heat and beat in flour and brandy until smooth. Drop the batter by a scant teaspoonful on a buttered baking sheet, leaving 4 inches between cookies. Bake only 4 at a time—more will cool before they can be rolled.

Bake in 325 degree oven for 10 minutes. If cookies are underbaked they will shrivel; if they cook too long they will be too brittle to roll. After removing from oven let cookies cool for about 30 seconds before removing one at a time from baking sheet with a spatula. Roll each around a wooden broom handle, or form into a cornucopia. For the latter, drape the warm cookie over the handle of a pot briefly until it is cool enough to handle. Then form into a cone shape and hold or prop until set. If cookies cool before they can be shaped, return them briefly to oven. Makes about 2 dozen.

Love Letters

No mistaking the message of these tender missives sealed with a red cinnamon heart. For fun, leave a few of the flaps open and, instead of jam, tuck a Victorian sonnet inside the edible envelope.

>4 tablespoons butter, softened
>4 ounces cream cheese
>1 cup cake flour
>2 tablespoons confectionery sugar
>Jam

Using an electric mixer or processor, cream butter and cream cheese until smooth. Spread mixture on the bottom of a large, wide bowl. Sift flour and confectionery sugar onto mixture. Gently knead with hands until blended. Minimal handling of this dough while blending and rolling is necessary to produce tender cookies.

Divide dough into 2 parts. Flatten one onto a sheet of waxed paper about 16 inches long. (Dough should be extremely soft but not sticky. If sticky, dust waxed paper with flour before placing dough on it.) Cover with another sheet of waxed paper. With a rolling pin spread dough out almost to edges forming a rectangle about 10 × 13 inches. Trim edges. Transfer dough and papers to a baking sheet and chill in refrigerator for an hour or two. Carefully remove top paper, turn dough upside down onto baking sheet, remove other paper and dough is ready to be shaped directly on the baking sheet.

Cut into 2½-inch squares. Put a tiny dab of jam on each square and fold in the corners to form an envelope. If dough becomes too soft while working with it return it briefly to refrigerator. Seal the top flap, if desired, with a red cinnamon heart. Repeat rolling and shaping steps for other half of dough.

Bake in 350 degree oven for 15 minutes or until edges are just beginning to color. Transfer to a rack to cool. Makes about 36 Love Letters.

Trilbys

No doubt these cookies were named for the beauty who abandoned her life as an artist's model when she fell under the spell of Svengali.

These old-fashioned sour cream cookies have a very tender crumb. With bright red raspberry jam peeking out through the top they are a grand choice to serve for an intimate tête à tête.

⅓ cup butter
½ cup sugar
1 egg
1 teaspoon vanilla
2 cups flour, scant
½ teaspoon baking powder
¼ teaspoon baking soda
⅓ cup sour cream
Raspberry jam

Cream butter and sugar until light and fluffy. Beat in the egg and vanilla. Sift together the flour, baking powder and soda. Add to butter mixture alternately with the sour cream and mix until thoroughly blended. Divide into two and wrap each in plastic wrap. Refrigerate overnight or for at least 3 hours.

As dough is very soft, alternate working with the portions, leaving one in refrigerator while working with the other. Form scraps into a flattened ball and return to refrigerator between cutting and baking.

Roll dough out to ¼-inch thickness. With a 2½-inch round cutter cut cookies. Place half of the cookies on buttered baking sheet and spread with a half teaspoon of raspberry jam, spreading it out to within ½ inch of edge. Prepare top halves by stamping out a small circle in the center of each, or make an X in the center of each, spreading it open when it is in place to expose the jam.

Gently stretch and press the top cookie over and around the edge of the bottom cookie.

Bake in 350 degree oven for 15 minutes or until edges begin to color. Remove immediately from baking sheet and cool on rack. Makes about 2 dozen Trilbys.

Chocolate Cake

This is a sweetheart of a chocolate cake—rich and moist, not too sugary. It is the perfect recipe for a fretful cook. Will the cake rise? This one will and then it will fall, as it is supposed to. For the indecisive cook who can't decide on what frosting to use, and for the harried cook with little time, the frosting is a portion of the batter held out from the baking to be spread on later. There is no flour in the batter but there is a cupful of nuts.

> ½ cup butter
> 6 ounces semi-sweet chocolate
> 9 egg yolks (have eggs at room temperature)
> 1 cup confectionery sugar
> 1 teaspoon vanilla
> 1 cup finely ground pecans (4 ounces)
> 7 egg whites
> 2 tablespoons granulated sugar
> Pistachio nuts for trim

Put butter, cut into pieces, and chocolate in a pan over simmering water to melt. Separate eggs. (Because of the large quantity used, separate them first into small bowls before transferring them into larger bowls; if a yolk breaks all will not be lost.) Remove the first two whites from sight to avoid confusion. When chocolate and butter are completely melted, stir to blend and remove from heat to cool.

Beat egg yolks lightly with a whisk, then blend in confectionery sugar. Add vanilla and mix in well. Stir cooled chocolate mixture gently into egg yolk mixture. Remove ⅔ cup of batter to be used as frosting and refrigerate it until needed. Stir ground pecans thoroughly into remaining batter.

Whip egg whites until foamy. Gradually add granulated sugar and beat until stiff. Fold into the chocolate mixture. Bake in a buttered 9-inch springform pan in 350 degree oven for 45 minutes. Center should spring back when touched. Run a knife completely around the edge to loosen cake from pan so it will fall evenly. Cool cake completely on a rack. Remove from pan and place on a cake dish.

Frost top and sides with reserved batter/frosting. With a peeler, make shavings of pistachios and sprinkle on top. Although this is a single-layer cake it is compact and rich and so will serve 10.

VIII

Breakfast
in Scotland

Oatmeal Bread
Orange Marmalade
Scots Eggs
Woodcock
Scones
Clotted Cream
Black Bun
Shortbread
Petticoat Tails
Gingerbread Husbands
Butterscotch

Samuel Johnson concluded after his travels that in all the world it was to Scotland he would go for breakfast. Recommendation enough to assemble this sampling of bonnie recipes. Here are the makings of a grand spread—minus the Sheeps Head and Haggis. Slide the time down from breakfast to brunch and practice some good northern country hospitality.

Start with a warm savory—Woodcock and a platter of Scots Eggs accompanied by the famous Scones, soft and white and served with cream and Orange Marmalade. Borrowing from the country's most traditional food, offer a hefty, healthful Oatmeal Bread. To keep company, add a good fat cheese and lumps of yellow butter. For what Sir Walter Scott called nonsense sweet things and confections with whim-whams, set out Shortbread and fruity Black Bun. Finally, pass around a plate of Gingerbread Husbands and some home-made Butterscotch. Only with reluctance were the old Scottish reckonings in the recipes changed to cups and pints from tassie, mutchkins and choppins.

The table is spread with a plaid cloth, painted bowls and jugs, a pewter plate or two. Pull up to the table the creepies or stools and boil a large quantity of water for tea. Some of the water will be needed to "beam the teapot" (rinse it with hot water before brewing). A hearty brew of tea will be welcomed to wash down the wholesome fare. Recommended is Chinese Keemun. Often called English Breakfast, it is sometimes not truly a blend at all but straight Keemun. With its thick full liquor and rich penetrating aroma, it is called the burgundy of China teas. Milk—there's no place for lemon here—and sugar set out.

A teapot blessed with a generous girth is needed for this occasion, as old Scotch hospitality considered it impolite to refill one cup until all cups were ready for another go-around.

After second and third helpings, when appetites have slowed, when contentment rises to the ceiling like the smoke from a peat fire, when not another bite can be managed, it is customary for the hostess to assume a thick, rolling burr and scold the guests, "Och, sich a porrr tea you've taken."

Oatmeal Bread

From the land of the oats, a recipe for bread that makes a good plump loaf which fairly demands to be cut in thick slices. Molasses, or treacle, gives the bread a bit of a burr.

1½ cups rolled oats
1 tablespoon molasses
1 tablespoon honey
2 teaspoons salt
2 cups boiling water
1 tablespoon butter
1 package dry yeast
¼ cup warm water (115 degrees)
4 cups white flour, approximately

Mix the oats, molasses, salt, butter and boiling water in a large bowl and stir well. Mash out any lumps with back of wooden spoon. Soften yeast in water. Stir the flour into the oat mixture. Add the yeast mixture. Knead well and then place in a greased bowl set over a bowl of hot water. Cover with towel and let it rise until about doubled. Punch dough down and knead lightly into a loaf. Place in greased pan. Brush top of loaf with water and sprinkle with a handful of oatmeal. Cover and let it rise again until dough reaches top of pan. Bake in a 350 degree oven for at least one hour. Crust should be browned and sound hollow when thumped on bottom.

Orange Marmalade

One would think oranges grew in Scotland, so closely is the country associated with orange marmalade. With the weather so often drizzly and dreary, it is not difficult to imagine the delight in a marmalade that seems to capture sunshine in a jar. Oranges from Seville—with a bitter flavor—are most prized, especially in the town of Dundee where the Keiller Family has been making marmalade from them since the early 18th century.

This recipe calls for only two oranges. It makes a quantity small enough to be stored in the refrigerator for some weeks, and so dispenses with directions for sterilizing and such.

> 2 medium oranges
> ½ lemon
> 3 cups water
> 2 cups sugar

Wash the oranges and lemon and put them whole into a large enamel or stainless saucepan. Add the water, cover and simmer for an hour. Cool, cut fruits in half, then squeeze the juice out and strain it into the saucepan with the remaining liquid. Boil for 10 minutes. Scrape membrane and white pulp from inside orange skins and discard along with the half lemon. Cut peels into matchstick-sized slices.

Add cut rind to the saucepan, then stir in sugar. Stir until mixture boils and sugar is dissolved. Now let mixture bubble without stirring on as high a heat as it can without boiling over, for 20 minutes or until a candy thermometer registers 220 degrees. Remove from heat. With a spoon skim off the foam on the surface. Ladle into a preserve jar or into Great Grandmother's best cut glass jam jar. If rind rises while cooling, stir it with a spoon to distribute throughout. Makes 1¾ cups.

Scots Eggs

"Will you no' take an egg te yer tea?" This question, put in a fine woolly brogue, is an invitation to eggs wrapped in sausage and baked. Serving an egg with tea was once considered a mark of prosperity. Today, it is still the sign of a generous host. This is a very delicious way to serve up two morning staples—eggs and sausage—in an unusual form. Small- or medium-sized eggs make servings just the right size. If large or jumbo eggs are used, slice them in half just before serving and "dish them up" cut side down.

    8 hard-boiled eggs
    1 pound ground pork sausage
    Flour to dust eggs
    1 egg, slightly beaten
    ½ cup fine breadcrumbs

Peel hard-boiled eggs. Divide sausage into 8 parts and flatten each into a round. Lightly coat eggs with flour. Shape a portion of sausage around each egg to completely enclose. Roll each in beaten egg and then in breadcrumbs, pressing crumbs well into the sausage. Bake on a rack in a shallow pan in 375 degree oven for 25 to 30 minutes. Serves 8.

Woodcock

The frugal Scotch housewife managed to serve the game bird woodcock by devising a dish that required no bird at all. It would more accurately—and truthfully—be named Mock Cock.

> 8 slices bread
> Butter
> Anchovy paste
> 4 tablespoons butter
> 2 eggs
> 6 egg yolks
> 1 cup cream
> ½ teaspoon salt
> Dash of cayenne pepper
> Capers

Toast bread, trim crusts and cut bread into triangles. Butter toast and spread with anchovy paste so thinly that its identity will be illusively imperceptible. Cover and keep warm.

In top of double boiler, over but not in simmering water, melt 4 tablespoons butter. Beat the eggs and yolks with the cream and stir into butter. Stir until thickened. If eggs begin to scramble, quickly lift pan from water and smooth mixture with a whisk. Season with salt and cayenne. Spoon over toast triangles and dot with capers. Serves 8.

Scones

Pronounced always in the Scottish way to rhyme with fawns and served always with tea. "Dropped Scones" refers not to a kitchen accident, but to a way of preparing them—poured or dropped on a girdle, not a griddle. Oven baking is today's preferred method. Like its first cousin, the muffin, scone dough must be handled minimally and quickly. As soon as the soda makes contact with liquid the rising action has begun—the object is to get the scones into the oven quickly while the dough is still wobbling so the rising is not wasted.

Although there are countless recipes for Scones this one goes back to basics for 3 simple ingredients—self-rising flour, buttermilk and soda. (Self-rising flour may be replaced by all-purpose flour sifted with 3 teaspoons of baking powder.) The buttermilk reacting with the soda produces a light, soft crumb. Although other recipes may call for cream or treacle or butter or eggs, a pure and simple recipe is best for starters. After all, Scones are nothing more than an airy excuse for jam and cream. Old Scotch scone saying: Prepared swiftly, served promptly, scones disappear quickly.

2 cups self-rising flour
½ teaspoon baking soda
¾ cup buttermilk
Milk or egg for glaze, if desired

Heat oven to 350 degrees. Sift self-rising flour at least once into mixing bowl. Stir soda into buttermilk until it begins to foam. Pour into well in center of flour and stir with fork incorporating just enough flour to make a very soft dough. Gather into ball and place on lightly floured board. Pat or roll into a circle, kneading very lightly. Use spatula to cut into 8 or 10 wedges. Transfer to greased baking sheet. To give Scones a shine, brush with milk; for a golden gleam brush with an egg yolk beaten with a tablespoon of water.

Bake for 10 to 12 minutes in upper third of oven. Wrap in linen napkin, tuck into basket and serve soon. Makes 8 to 10 Scones.

Clotted Cream

A traditional accompaniment to scones, clotted cream is a result of long and careful warming and skimming. Its butterfat content is so high that only a fine line distinguishes it from butter. Without a cow of one's own it is difficult to make real clotted cream—the homogenization and pasteurization of dairy processing get in the way. A substitute may be made by whipping a pint of heavy cream just to the point of stiffness and heaviness. Store in refrigerator but serve at room temperature heaped in a bowl.

Black Bun

Black Bun is the marvelous but inaccurate name for an esteemed Scotch treat. Neither bun, pie nor cake, it is best described as fruit and cake baked in a crust. So heavy with fruit, it was once described as being as hard to pick up as a Glasgow drunk on a Saturday night. Although the finished product is a real Busby Berkeley production, preparations can be handled in segments. The pastry, for example, can be made ahead and kept waiting in the refrigerator, or store-bought unbaked pie shells may be used. The fruit and nut mixture may be prepared and measured and then set aside—for days, if kept hidden from nibblers. If possible, Black Bun should be made a few weeks before serving so that it can sit and hum awhile. It is said to last up to a year if kept in an airtight tin—but who would have the willpower to find that out?

Pastry

¼ cup lard
¼ cup butter
2 cups flour
¼ to ½ cup ice water

Cut shortening into flour in small pieces. Blend together with pastry cutter or fork until mixture becomes mealy. Add ice water gradually while stirring with fork until ball can be formed. Wrap in plastic and place in refrigerator while preparing filling.

Filling

1 cup pitted prunes
1 cup figs
2 apples
1 orange
2 cups currants
2 cups raisins
¼ pound candied peel
½ cup chopped almonds
2½ cups flour
1 teaspoon baking powder
1 cup sugar
1 teaspoon black pepper, finely ground
1 teaspoon allspice
1 teaspoon cinnamon
2 eggs, lightly beaten
⅓ cup milk
⅓ cup brandy

Chop prunes and figs. Core and peel apples, wash orange, remove seeds, and cut apples and oranges into chunks. Use food processor, blender or grinder to chop coarsely. Thoroughly mix together currants, raisins, prunes, figs, candied peel, almonds, apples and orange in bowl and set aside.

Sift together flour, baking powder, sugar, pepper, allspice and cinnamon. Combine eggs, milk and brandy and stir into dry mixture. Add fruit and nut mixture and combine well.

On lightly floured board, roll out ⅔ of pastry dough into a circle large enough to cover the bottom and sides of an 8-inch springform pan. Arrange pastry in pan and smooth against bottom and sides. Fill with fruit batter. Roll remaining pastry into an 8-inch-diameter circle and place on top of cake. Cut off ragged edges from bottom crust and seal edges of top and bottom using fingertips moistened with water. Use large skewer or chopstick to form 6 holes extending down from top through batter to bottom pastry.

Place in center of 275 degree oven. Bake for 30 minutes. Reduce oven temperature to 225 degrees and bake for 2½ more hours. If top has not browned, brush with milk and return to oven for 5 minutes more or until browned. Cool in pan for ½ hour.

If Black Bun is to be stored for any length of time, brandy may be dripped into top holes for added moisture and flavor. For longtime keeping, store in tin or cake keeper.

Shortbread

Shortbread is the delicious culinary synergism which results from the blending of 3 very basic ingredients—butter, flour and sugar.

1 cup sweet butter
⅔ cup sugar (preferably superfine)
3 cups white flour, approximately

Cut 2 sticks of butter into a large mixing bowl. With mixer, whip butter until it is creamy. Add sugar gradually and beat until light colored and fluffy.

Remove mixer and, using a wooden spoon, gently blend in the 3 cups of flour. Depending on the moisture in butter and flour this amount will be approximate, but the aim is to make a very "short" dough by using as little flour as possible.

Divide dough into 3 8-inch round pans and pat down smooth. Rolling and cutting are not necessary and should be avoided as they tend to toughen the dough. With a fluted pastry wheel or a fork divide each into 8 wedges.

Bake in center of 325 degree oven for 30 minutes or just until a hint of darkening begins to show around edges. When almost cool, break apart. If breaks are not clean, use fork to deepen the perforations. Warm briefly before serving. Makes 24.

Petticoat Tails

Petticoat Tails is the name given to shortbread cut in the shape of a skirt. To make, press dough into round pans as before. Press a round cookie cutter or a glass upside down into the center of the pan. Cut the outside circle into wedges. Break apart when slightly cooled as for shortbread.

Gingerbread Husbands

That's what gingerbread men are called in parts of Scotland. Don't bake them without trimming with black currants for face and buttons—they look undressed without.

> ¼ cup butter
> ½ cup brown sugar
> ½ cup molasses
> ⅓ cup water
> 3½ cups flour
> 1 teaspoon soda
> 2 teaspoons ginger
> ½ teaspoon each of salt, allspice, cloves and cinnamon
> Currants for trim

Mix butter, brown sugar and molasses thoroughly. Stir in water. Sift the flour, soda and spices together. Stir them into the liquid mixture. Add more water by drops if necessary. Refrigerate for several hours or overnight.

Roll dough approximately ¼-inch thick on lightly floured board. Cut with cutter. Place on lightly greased baking sheet. Press in currants for eyes, mouth and 3 buttons.

Bake in 350 degree oven for 10 minutes or until edges just begin to brown. Makes about 1 dozen fat Gingerbread Husbands.

Butterscotch

½ cup brown sugar
½ cup white sugar
¼ cup corn syrup
¼ cup butter
⅓ cup water
1 teaspoon lemon juice

Combine sugars, corn syrup, butter, water and lemon juice in a large, heavy pot. Boil, stirring constantly, until candy thermometer reaches 280 degrees or until a bit dropped in cold water forms a hard but not brittle thread—soft crack stage.

Remove from heat and pour into a buttered 8-inch square pan. Cool until it begins to harden. Mark into 1-inch squares. When set, break or cut along the scoring.

IX

The Tea Dance

Sandwiches
Cucumber, Radish, Smoked Salmon
Madeleines
Bourbon Balls
Cream Puffs
Jelly Rolls
Spiced Nuts
Fish House Punch
Gooseberry Fool

The time is late afternoon on a Sunday, after the polo match and the croquet tournament, when all have worked up ravenous appetites for cucumber sandwiches and other food fripperies.

In the throng around the punchbowl, the girls try not to crush their organdy dresses and one of the dandies offers his monogrammed silver flask for spiking.

When Emily Post wrote her first etiquette book in the 1920s, she laid down many rules concerning the serving and drinking of tea. One of them was how to answer a guest's request for a cup of tea. "Certainly!" was the correct response. Updated editions of her book still stand on that as the proper answer. In the years in between there have been legions of grateful hostesses who have depended on that bit of advice.

Today's tea dance menu may even dispense with the dispensing of hot tea. Pitchers of iced tea trimmed with fresh mint sprigs will be welcomed by the dancers working up a pretty "glow." And that veddy proper *thé dansant* standby, Fish House Punch, is, after all, made with a tea base.

The tea table is set as a buffet so that guests may help themselves. Additionally, maids and footmen may also circulate among the guests with trays of food. The menu might include Madeleines—very recherché, Brandy Balls, small Cream Puffs, Jelly Rolls, another tea dance standby, Gooseberry Fool, and silver bowls filled with Spiced Nuts. In addition to the Cucumber Sandwiches are other finger-sized sandwiches.

Mrs. Post suggested a screen of potted palms for the orchestra to sit behind. Potted palms are still a smashing addition—more likely now to conceal the stereo system which will be playing Lester Lanin recordings of Cole Porter songs, just the right tempo for the fox trot—danced with plenty of dips and arm pumping.

Sandwiches

Cucumber sandwiches are essential to the tea dance menu. Add smoked salmon and radish sandwiches for a most harmonious trio.

The general consensus on quantities needed is that two slices of bread with a filling will make about 4 tiny sandwiches—

an adequate serving for one. An adequate serving, provided there are lots of other good cakes and cookies to sample.

Cucumber Sandwiches

    1 large cucumber
    Salt
    ½ cup mayonnaise
    1 loaf white bread, home-made style, thinly sliced
    White pepper

Peel cucumber. Cut lengthwise into quarters and remove seeds. Use a vegetable parer to cut paperthin lengthwise strips. Place in ice water with ½ teaspoon of salt. Soak for 15 minutes, then drain well and pat dry well with towels. Cut strips into bread-size lengths.

Spread mayonnaise on each slice of bread. Cover half of the slices with overlapping strips of cucumber. Sprinkle lightly with white pepper. Top each with a slice of bread. Press together lightly. Trim off crusts. Cut each sandwich into four fingers. Cover with a damp towel and refrigerate until serving time. Makes about 32.

Radish Sandwiches

The directions for cucumber sandwiches specify mayonnaise as the spread although it must be recognized that there is a sizable butter-not-mayonnaise claque. Radish sandwiches, however, require butter, sweet butter, not salted, and never margarine, for a certain culinary alchemy to occur. Radish sandwiches, properly made, taste like something else—and they can become addictive.

    1 bunch of radishes
    1 loaf white bread, thinly sliced
    6 tablespoons sweet butter, softened
    Salt

Wash radishes well and cut off stem ends. Slice very thinly in circles. Spread each slice of bread with butter. Trim off crusts. Cut each into four squares. Overlap radish circles on buttered bread so that a red edging shows between the slices. Sprinkle with salt. Cover with top slices of bread and press lightly together. Cover with a damp towel and refrigerate until serving time. Makes about 32.

Smoked Salmon Sandwiches
1 loaf pumpernickel or rye bread, thinly sliced
½ cup mayonnaise
½ pound smoked salmon, sliced paper thin
Freshly ground black pepper

Trim crusts from bread. Spread each slice with mayonnaise. Arrange sliced salmon on half the slices and sprinkle with freshly ground black pepper. Cover with another bread slice and cut into fingers or triangles. Cover with plastic wrap and refrigerate until serving time. Makes about 36.

Madeleines

No book about the good things to eat with tea would be complete without a recipe for these buttery little spongecakes. The French novelist Marcel Proust dunked a Madeleine into a cup of tea and was prompted to write a novel eight volumes long. Serve with caution to budding authors.

5 tablespoons butter
2 eggs, at room temperature
½ teaspoon vanilla
Rind of ½ lemon, finely grated
⅓ cup sugar
½ cup flour
Pinch of salt

Prepare scallop-shaped Madeleine pans before mixing batter. Use additional butter to that called for in recipe and butter the molds most carefully with an even coating. Use softened but not melted butter. Sprinkle molds with flour and shake out excess by tapping firmly on counter. Madeleine molds come in small and large sizes. This recipe will make approximately 40 small or 20 large Madeleines. In lieu of metal molds, real sea shells may be used—either gathered from the beach or bought in kitchen-ware stores. Butter and flour them as directed and place them on a baking sheet.

Melt 5 tablespoons of butter and set aside after skimming and discarding foam from top.

Heat oven to 350 degrees.

In a small bowl beat eggs with an electric mixer until they are thick and lemon-colored. Add the vanilla and lemon rind. While beating, gradually add the sugar. Beat for 15 minutes or until quite thick.

On low speed, gradually beat in flour which has been sifted with salt. Stop beating as soon as flour is incorporated. Quickly fold in the melted butter until just blended. Immediately spoon batter into prepared molds filling them to the top. (This must be done quickly before butter begins to separate from batter.) Bake for 15 minutes or until they are golden. Remove cookies from shells after cooling for a minute or two and place them on a rack to finish cooling.

Bourbon Balls

2 cups cookie crumbs (or Graham Cracker crumbs, or
    toasted cake crumbs)
2 tablespoons cocoa
1 cup confectionery sugar
1 cup chopped walnuts
2 tablespoons light corn syrup
⅓ cup bourbon
Cocoa

Crush crumbs finely in blender. Mix crumbs, cocoa, confectionery sugar and nuts. Stir corn syrup into bourbon and mix well. Add to dry ingredients and mix well with hands. Roll into long log shape. Cut into 36 pieces. Roll each piece into a ball. Roll each in cocoa.

Keep in a tin box—flavor improves with a few days of aging.

This recipe makes 3 dozen. Recipe may be doubled but add liquid slowly, stopping as soon as dough holds together.

Cream Puffs

Choux pastry, which is what cream puffs are made from, is like an edible, all-occasion gift-wrapping. The name chou, which is French for little cabbage, comes from the cream puff's resemblance to that lowly vegetable. But the resemblance is all that is humble about the pastry. It takes on many delightful identities. It makes the tall pyramidal croquembouche, elongated éclairs, delicate cream-filled swans. With the elimination of sugar from its ingredients, choux pastry can become a case for hors d'oeuvre or savories.

Here, for an occasion involving the balancing of a tea cup while sipping and eating simultaneously, the recipe is for miniature one-bite cream puffs.

1 cup water
½ cup butter
1 tablespoon sugar
½ teaspoon salt
1 cup flour
4 eggs, at room temperature

Place water in a saucepan and cut the butter into it. Add sugar and salt and stir over heat. When the mixture comes to a full boil, lower heat, add flour all at once and stir rapidly until mixture leaves sides of pan and forms a smooth, stiff ball. Remove from heat and allow to sit for a few minutes.

If processor is available, transfer mixture to it—it guarantees an exceptional puff—and process for 15 seconds. Add the eggs and process about 30 seconds until dough is shiny.

Otherwise, add eggs one at a time, beating until mixture is smooth after each addition; it will become very thick.

Transfer mixture to pastry bag fitted with ½-inch tip. Pipe out rounds of dough about 1 inch across onto lightly greased baking sheet. Hold tip on sheet allowing paste to billow up around it into round shape. Leave room between for puffs to spread out. Smooth out peaks with a wet fingertip.

Bake in 400 degree oven for 15 minutes or until puffed, very lightly browned and dry. They will collapse if underbaked. Immediately, prick hole in bottom of each to allow steam to escape. Place on rack to cool. Makes 3 to 4 dozen puffs.

Cream Puff Filling
2 cups heavy or whipping cream
⅓ cup confectionery sugar
2 teaspoons vanilla
Confectionery sugar

Whip cream in a cold, deep bowl, with sugar and vanilla, until firm. Just before serving, slice the tops off the cream puffs with a sharp knife and fill to overflowing with whipped cream. Press tops back on lightly so that a ruff of cream shows all around. When all are filled, sift additional confectionery sugar over the tops of all.

Or make a small hole in each puff and pipe in the whipped cream using a pastry bag.

Instead of whipped cream, the puffs may be filled with custard using the recipe for Trifle on page 20.

Jelly Rolls

Most Jelly Roll recipes direct the rolling to begin from the short side of the sponge cake which results in fewer, but larger, slices. For a tea such as this with an embarrassment of good things to sample, roll the sponge along the long side for more miniature-sized servings.

6 egg yolks
¼ cup water
1 cup sugar
Grated rind of one lemon
1½ cups cake flour
Pinch of salt
6 egg whites
Confectionery sugar for dusting
½ cup jelly (or more, to suit)

Prepare pan by buttering an 11- by 17-inch pan. Line it with a sheet of buttered and floured waxed paper.

In a large bowl, beat the egg yolks until thick and lemon colored. Add water and continue beating until very thick. Gradually beat in one half of the sugar. Add grated lemon rind. While continuing to beat on low speed, gradually sift the flour and salt onto yolk mixture until batter is smooth.

With clean beaters, whip egg whites until soft peaks form. Add the remaining half cup of sugar gradually and beat until the mixture is shiny. Fold egg whites into batter quickly, combining them gently but thoroughly. With a rubber spatula smooth batter onto prepared pan.

Bake in 375 degree oven for 10 to 12 minutes or until cake begins to color and it springs back to the touch. Do not overbake or cake will crack when rolled.

Remove from oven and sprinkle top of cake with a thin coating of confectionery sugar. Place a damp but well wrung-out kitchen towel over cake and turn upside down onto counter top. Let cool for 5 minutes. Remove pan, then carefully peel off paper. With a sharp knife trim off the four edges of the cake. Roll up (towel and all) very tightly beginning with a long edge. Let sit in refrigerator until chilled and set. Unroll and remove towel.

Warm the jelly. (No pale jellies wanted here. Use a bright red or purple that will stand out from the pale cake.) Spread it evenly on the roll with a pastry brush. Roll up snugly and place seam down. Slice thinly and arrange on a cake plate. Makes 24 Jelly Rolls.

Spiced Nuts

1 egg white
1 teaspoon water
1 cup whole almonds, blanched
1 cup pecan halves
½ cup sugar
½ teaspoon salt
1 teaspoon cinnamon
½ teaspoon nutmeg
½ teaspoon ground ginger

Beat egg white with water until frothy. Add nuts and stir until each nut is well coated. Mix sugar, salt, cinnamon, nutmeg and ginger in another bowl. Toss nuts in sugar and spice mixture and mix well. Spread the nuts on large enough baking sheet so that they are not crowded. Bake in 225 degree oven for 1 hour, stirring the mixture every 15 minutes. Remove nuts from pan and shake off loose sugar.

Fish House Punch

If serving on a very hot afternoon, make up the punch in pitchers and store in refrigerator until serving time. Keep some in refrigerator and replenish punch bowl as needed.

1 quart strong tea
2 cups lemon juice
1½ cups sugar
2 fifths rum
1 fifth brandy or cognac
1 pint peach brandy

Pour tea and lemon juice into a punch bowl, add sugar and stir to dissolve. Pour in rum, brandy and peach brandy. Mix well.

Place a large block of ice in the center of bowl. Allow punch to chill well. Stir before serving. Serve in punch glasses. Makes 4½ quarts or 36 4-ounce servings.

Gooseberry Fool

For five centuries this has been an English favorite. Puréed fruit swirled with whipped cream, it is simplicity itself to make. The only difficulty may be in obtaining the uncommon gooseberry. Canned gooseberries may be used instead of fresh. From New Zealand comes another entry in the world of gooseberries—they are the color and size of red grapes but cook to a cheery bright red. The newly popular kiwi fruit—appropriately called the Chinese gooseberry—is the same bright green as the original and makes a fine substitute. They too may be treated like gooseberries—peeled, in this case—simmered and strained. Or they may be left unstrained and their tiny black seeds left in for a bit of crunch. Then too, the kiwis may be mashed and used uncooked. Some say there's no Fool like a fresh Fool!

> 1 quart gooseberries
> ½ cup sugar (or more to taste)
> 2 cups whipping cream

If using fresh gooseberries, cook them in a saucepan over low heat for 20 minutes. Mash some in the beginning to extract a bit of juice, or add a tablespoon of water. When gooseberries have softened, stir in sugar. If they have not cooked to a thick pulp at the end of the cooking time, boil briefly to reduce. (Purée will thicken with chilling.) Refrigerate until cold.

Just before serving, whip cream until stiff. Place in a glass bowl or compote. Fold gooseberry purée into the cream just enough to create a marbled effect. Set out small individual glass bowls or punch cups and let guests help themselves. Makes 8 to 10 small but surfeiting servings.

X

Hearthside Tea in an Irish Kitchen

Soda Bread
Rum Butter
Plum Jam
Porter Cake
Lemon Curd Tartlets
Boxties
Oatmeal Cookies
Yellowman

Spread the table with a linen cloth of the woven, checkered variety, not the good damask, and set out an earthenware teapot and sturdy mugs. This spot of tea is meant to be dawdled over, so the perfect accessory to keep the teapot steaming is a tea cozy.

An open fire is a fine addition to the scene and a cat is a fine addition to the hearth. The two most soothing sounds in the world may be the hissing of the tea kettle and the purring of a cat. An apple peel simmering with a cinnamon stick and a few cloves adds an evocative fragrance to the air.

The Irish love a robust and pungent type of tea, so Irish Breakfast Tea is a classic choice. It is a blend of high-grown Ceylon and hearty Indian Assam—both black teas. It is a heart-warming, wake-up tea and a good blend to put milk in. Obviously, the Irish did not name it Breakfast Tea, for they don't stop drinking it then but enjoy it throughout the day.

The cook in an Irish kitchen must always remember to stir ingredients clockwise—to humor the Druids. That holds true for Soda Bread, Boxties, Oatmeal Cookies and all the other good recipes that follow.

A sampling of these recipes served mid-morning is a lovely way to welcome a new neighbor or to renew acquaintance with an old.

Soda Bread

It originally was a round loaf baked in a covered iron pot suspended over the fire. When baked this way it likes glowing embers on top of its lid to give all-around heat. If baking this bread over an open fire, lift the cover occasionally and baste the top of the loaf with butter. If using an oven, turn the temperature to 375 degrees and bake the loaf on a baking sheet. Before baking, cut a cross on the top with a knife to let the devil out. (This also lets the loaf expand without cracking.)

2 cups flour
1 teaspoon baking soda
1 teaspoon baking powder
½ teaspoon salt
1 tablespoon sugar
6 tablespoons butter
¾ cup buttermilk

Sift the flour, baking soda, baking powder, salt and sugar into a big bowl. Cut the butter into small pieces and rub it into the dry ingredients with fingertips until the mixture looks like cornmeal. Add most of the buttermilk, beating quickly with a large wooden spoon. Mix until a ball is formed, adding more buttermilk by the spoonful, as needed. Put the dough on a lightly floured surface and pat into a roundish loaf. Put the loaf on a buttered baking sheet and bake in 375 degree oven for 40 minutes or until loaf is well browned.

To make the Irish version of Spotted Dog, simply follow the recipe for Soda Bread but toss into the sifted dry ingredients a half cupful of black currants or raisins.

Rum Butter and Plum Jam make fine accompaniments to Soda Bread.

Rum Butter

½ cup sweet butter
⅓ cup superfine sugar
1 teaspoon cinnamon
1 teaspoon orange rind, finely grated
¼ cup dark rum

Whip the butter until fluffy. Blend in sugar, cinnamon, orange rind and rum. Pack the mixture into a crock and place it in a cool spot until it firms a bit.

Plum Jam

Use any variety of plum for this. Each produces its own distinctive flavor and color.

1 pound of plums
1 cup sugar
Lemon juice (add 1 tablespoon to fruit and sugar mixture if plums
　　are not of a tart variety)

　　Cut plums in half and discard pits. Place cut side down in a pan and cook over low heat until juice coats the pot bottom. Raise heat and simmer until plums are softened. Put plums through a sieve or food processor or blender.

　　Measure one cup of plum purée and one cup of sugar and return to pan. Let mixture come to a boil slowly, stirring until sugar is dissolved. Cook at a moderate boil for 30 minutes, stirring occasionally to make sure fruit does not stick or scorch. Cool slightly and pour into a jam jar.

Porter Cake

From Glengarriff, in County Cork, here's a great grandmotherly recipe. This cake was formerly made with porter—which has now been phased out in favor of stout—the richest, heaviest and darkest of beers and one of the most potent. The Irish claim that stout is good for a person; it certainly is good for this cake. It gives a fine "winy" flavor to it.

　　The recipe calls for mixed spice—a blend of ground spices commonly used in the British Isles. It is made of cinnamon, nutmeg, mace, cloves, coriander and caraway or ginger. A homemade blend can be prepared balancing proportions to the cook's taste. Or more simply, use allspice, the berry of the Pimenta tree, which resembles the combined flavors of these spices.

> 4 cups self-rising flour
> ½ teaspoon salt
> 2 cups sugar
> ½ teaspoon ground nutmeg
> ½ teaspoon ground mixed spice
> 1 cup butter
> 2 ounces chopped mixed fruit peel
> 1 pound golden raisins
> 2 ounces glacé cherries, halved
> 1 cup stout, often called Guinness
> 2 eggs, beaten

Sift together flour, salt, sugar, nutmeg and spice. Cut in butter and rub in finely. Add fruits. Add stout mixed with beaten eggs. Bake in a well-greased tube pan for 2½ hours in a 300 degree oven. Makes 24 or more servings.

Lemon Curd Tartlets

Throughout the United Kingdom lemon curd ranks as an all-time, old time favorite. Besides being a scrumptious tart filling, it is delicious as a spread for toast—small wonder since its ingredients are pure butter, sugar, eggs and lemon.

> *Lemon Curd*
> 2 whole eggs
> 2 yolks
> ½ cup sugar
> ⅓ cup fresh lemon juice
> ¼ cup butter

In the top of a double boiler combine eggs and yolks and beat lightly. Mix in sugar and lemon juice. Place over simmering water and cook, stirring constantly, for about 5 minutes until mixture thickens. Do not let mixture boil; it will curdle. Remove pan from hot water and cut butter into mixture. Stir until butter is melted. Lemon curd will thicken more when refrigerated. Makes 1½ cups.

Pastry for Tartlets

2 tablespoons sugar
1 cup flour
½ cup vegetable oil
3 to 4 tablespoons ice water

Stir sugar into flour. Blend in vegetable oil. Stir in water. Work the pastry briefly with hands and form into ball.

Tart and tartlet forms—also called teacake, gem and patty pans—come in almost as many sizes and shapes as there are varieties of fillings for them. And there are almost as many methods for fitting pastry into the shells. One method is to cut circles out of the rolled-out pastry dough and fit them into the inside of the shells. Another is to work with the tart tin upside down and fit the circle of pastry around the outside of the form. Another way is to pinch off a ball of pastry and mold it on the inside bottom of the shell and up around the sides. Probably the simplest is this fourth method: roll out dough to a rectangle the size of the whole tin. Drape it over the top and cut through it around the individual shells. Work the pastry down inside the shells and cut off excess dough cleanly with a knife.

For delicacy's sake, the dough should be rolled out no more than ⅛-inch thick. The tinier the tart, the thinner the crust ought to be.

When shells have been formed, prick bottom and sides well with a fork. Bake in 375 degree oven for 12 to 18 minutes or until the edges are lightly browned. Length of baking depends on size of tarts; the smaller the tart, the shorter the time. Allow the tart shells to cool before filling with chilled lemon curd.

Boxties

The boxty is a traditional potato cake that sometimes is baked, sometimes griddled. This recipe makes them on a griddle so they resemble pancakes. Serve them hot, spread with butter and sprinkled with sugar. Or top them with nutmeg-dusted apple-sauce.

1 cup grated raw potatoes (one large baking potato)
½ cup flour
¼ cup milk
¼ cup melted butter
⅛ teaspoon salt

Peel and grate the potatoes. A mature baking type works best. Put grated potatoes on a cotton kitchen towel and wring tightly to remove as much liquid as possible. Put the potatoes in a bowl, toss with flour, add milk, butter and salt and stir the batter well. Grease a hot griddle and spoon batter onto it, forming small pancakes. Flip over once when bottom is golden brown. Makes a dozen 3-inch Boxties.

Oatmeal Cookies

To fill in the empty spaces, here is an exceptional recipe for oatmeal cookies. This will make about 25 soul-satisfying, chewy, good-textured cookies.

> ½ cup raisins
> ½ cup orange juice
> 1 egg
> ½ cup butter, melted
> ½ teaspoon vanilla
> 1 cup flour
> ½ teaspoon baking soda
> ¼ cup brown sugar
> 1 cup rolled oats

Put raisins into a small saucepan with orange juice and bring to a boil. Remove from heat and let them sit to plump while mixing other ingredients.

Beat egg lightly in mixing bowl. Add melted butter and vanilla and beat for a few minutes. Stir the flour, soda and sugar together. Add to the liquid mixture and beat until smooth. Drain raisins and stir them in; add the oats and mix well. Drop by rounded teaspoonsful onto buttered cookie sheets. Bake in 350 degree oven for 12 to 15 minutes or until lightly browned.

For big cookies, drop by heaping tablespoonsful and bake about 2 minutes longer. Makes about 1½ dozen large cookies.

For crispy cookies, cool completely on raised rack. For soft, chewy cookies, cool cookies directly on counter top, then pack airtight.

Yellowman

For over 350 years this brittle toffee has been sold at the Lammas Fair in Ballycastle, where it is chipped from large blocks with a hammer. For neater indoor serving, it may be poured into a buttered tin and cut into squares before it hardens.

1 tablespoon butter
¾ cup corn syrup
½ cup brown sugar
1 teaspoon water
1 tablespoon vinegar
½ teaspoon baking soda

Use a heavy saucepan large enough to contain the hot syrup when it foams up. Melt the butter and coat the bottom of the pan with it. Add corn syrup, brown sugar, water and vinegar. Stir just to blend, then let mixture boil without stirring until it reaches the hard crack stage—300 degrees on a candy thermometer or when a bit dropped into a cup of cold water becomes a brittle thread. Stir in the soda and pour onto a buttered marble slab, or onto a scrubbed and buttered formica counter top. Push the edges into the center with a sturdy spatula. When the mass has cooled enough to be handled, it may be pulled—find a friend with buttered hands to help. Or pour the hot mass into a buttered 8-inch square cake pan. Score into squares before it hardens. Break into squares when cool.

XI

A Garden Party

Fancy Sandwiches
Ribbon, Pinwheel, Asparagus Rolls

Chocolate Bread

Vanilla Butter

Angel Cake

Rose Icing

Petit Fours
Fondant Icing

Crystallized Flowers

Jam Creams

A wedding reception, a bridal shower, the blooming of the first of the summer lilies—all are valid reasons to hold a Garden Party. There may be a tent with a floor for dancing, catered umbrella tables and an orchestra—or just a picnic table covered with a pastel sheet and a lace-over cloth to set the scene.

The menu includes only foods that are fresh and beautiful to look at. Chocolate Bread with a bowl of Vanilla Butter to spread on it. Finger Sandwiches fashioned in ribbon stripes and pinwheels with pastel cream cheese fillings. Jam Creams, an Angel Cake with Rose Icing and Petit Fours glazed with Fondant Icing and trimmed with Crystallized Flowers.

If the tea is to be of a ceremonious nature, given to honor a celebrity or a debutante, refreshments are served in the dining room. For simpler teas, once known as lawn parties, food is served out of doors. The blended Earl Grey is a lovely tea with an affinity for desserts. Its piquant, bloomy aroma comes in part from the bergamot—a citric-rind oil—with which it is flavored. The best blends of Earl Grey contain China black and Darjeeling leaves.

Pitchers of iced tea are served if the day is very warm. There are two good methods for making iced tea, which must be clear and unclouded. One way is to fill a quart container—preferably glass as some metals cause clouding—with cold tap water. Remove the tags from 9 tea bags and let them brew in the water overnight at room temperature. For the other method, brew hot tea in the usual manner, using twice as much tea as would normally be used. This is to allow for dilution by ice. Allow it to stand for a half hour after steeping and then pour it into pitchers half filled with ice. Keemum tea is a good choice to use for this as it is known for its clarity. Serve the iced tea with lemon or mint leaves.

Fancy Sandwiches

Here are three classic Fancy Sandwiches—Ribbon, Pinwheel and Asparagus Rolls. Not surprisingly, they taste as good as they look. It is wise to set up some semblance of an assembly line. It will get them made quickly, will keep them from losing freshness and will enable them to look their best.

Ribbon Sandwiches
1 pound cream cheese, whipped
Black olives, pitted and finely minced
4 hardboiled egg yolks
½ avocado
Lemon juice
1 loaf white bread
1 loaf whole wheat bread
Parsley
Watercress

Divide the whipped cream cheese into four small bowls. Add minced olives to one and blend well to a creamy paste. Add mashed egg yolks to another and mashed avocado to the third, blending each well. Leave the cream cheese in the fourth bowl unmixed. Add a teaspoon of lemon juice to the avocado mixture to delay discoloring. If sandwiches must be made prior to the day of serving, substitute 2 tablespoons of finely minced fresh dill, parsley or watercress for the avocado.

Do not use thinly sliced bread for these sandwiches. They may be made with unsliced loaves cut lengthwise through in even slices, or with pre-sliced bread piled 5 slices high in mini-loaves. Spread the 4 cream cheese mixtures on the bread and stack them up, alternating brown slices with white. Press them firmly together, wrap airtight and chill. (Chill briefly in freezer for neater slicing.) Just before serving, trim off all crusts and slice the loaves into ½-inch slices. Cut each slice cross-wise in half. Arrange on trays garnished with sprigs of parsley and watercress. Makes about 3 dozen colorfully striped sandwiches.

Pinwheel Sandwiches
Red pimientos (from jar or can)
8 ounces whipped cream cheese
1 loaf white bread, unsliced

Drain as many pimientos as will equal approximately 2 tablespoons, minced. Chop them finely, or mash them with the back of a fork. Blend thoroughly with cream cheese.

Slice away the top and bottom and two end crusts from the loaf of bread, squaring it into a true rectangle. Cut slices the length of the loaf, ¼- to ½-inch thick. Spread each long slice with the cream cheese mixture. A narrow rubber spatula works well for spreading. Spread cheese well out to the edges so that roll will be well sealed. Starting at a short end, roll up each slice as for a jelly roll. Roll tightly. Put rolls snugly together, seam down, and wrap in dampened kitchen towel or plastic wrap.

Refrigerate until chilled and cylindrical shape has set. Trim crusts from ends and slice each roll crosswise into ½-inch wheels. Makes 10 to 12 rolls which may be sliced into 60 to 72 Pinwheels. Arrange on trays but cover airtight until serving time.

Asparagus Rolls
Canned asparagus works well for these sandwiches as the processing tenderizes the stalks, but only the best quality should be used. If using fresh asparagus be sure to remove the woody part of the stalk or pare with a peeler before cooking. This is one of those rare occasions when soft, commercial white bread can be recommended. It rolls up better than home-made style bread and its bland taste and texture, for a change, seem just right.

1 15-ounce can asparagus spears
1 loaf white bread
½ cup mayonnaise

Drain asparagus spears well. Salt and pepper, if desired. Cut crusts from bread. Spread with mayonnaise. Place an asparagus spear on each slice and roll up snugly, pressing end down securely. Wrap well in plastic wrap and keep in refrigerator until serving time. Makes 18 or more rolls.

Chocolate Bread

This is a real yeast bread but with a dark, deep chocolate soul. One bite is guaranteed to improve the disposition.

1 package dry yeast
¼ cup warm water (115 degrees)
1 tablespoon sugar
1 cup milk
2 tablespoons butter
⅓ cup sugar
1 teaspoon vanilla
2 eggs, beaten
3½ cups flour
½ cup cocoa
1 cup walnuts, chopped

Dissolve yeast in warm water with the tablespoon of sugar and set aside. Heat milk. Remove from heat and stir in butter until it melts. Add ⅓ cup sugar, vanilla and yeast mixture and stir. Add beaten eggs.

Measure flour into a large bowl. Stir the cocoa into it, blending well. Stir in nuts.

Combine yeast mixture with flour mixture and beat hard for two minutes with a wooden spoon. Let dough rest for 5 minutes. Turn out onto a lightly floured board and knead gently. Place ball into a buttered bowl and turn it, coating well. Cover with a damp towel and place in a warm place until doubled in size—about 2 hours.

Punch down and knead into loaf shape. Place in buttered loaf pan, cover again and let rise until doubled in size—about 1 hour.

Bake in 350 degree oven for about 1 hour. Halfway through the baking, place a piece of foil loosely over top of loaf to prevent crust from becoming too brown. Bread is done when it begins to pull away from sides of pan and it has filled the kitchen with the heady aroma of a chocolate factory. Let cool in pan for 10 minutes; remove from pan and cool on rack.

Serve with a bowl of Vanilla Butter nearby.

Vanilla Butter

8 tablespoons sweet butter
½ cup confectionery sugar
2 tablespoons vanilla extract

Cream the butter and sugar together until light and fluffy. Gradually beat in the vanilla extract until the mixture is smooth. Spoon into decorative serving bowl and chill until firm. Makes almost a cup.

For a more intense vanilla flavor, store confectionery sugar in a jar with a vanilla bean pod for a week before using.

Angel Cake

The full name is Angel Food Cake—so that's what angels eat. In the good old days a silver flatware service was not complete unless it included a long-pronged cutter designed especially for slicing Angel Cake. Those with a flair for the dramatic may instead use two forks held back to back to delicately "tear" slices. If using a knife, choose one with a serrated edge. This cake, which has a crumb as substantial as cotton candy, seems most suitable for a summer's afternoon tea party.

> 11 egg whites (or 1¼ cups)
> 1 cup sifted cake flour
> 1½ cups confectionery sugar
> ½ teaspoon salt
> 1 teaspoon cream of tartar
> 1 teaspoon vanilla
> ½ teaspoon almond extract

First prepare a 10-inch tube pan by scrubbing it out with detergent and rinsing it thoroughly. Any trace of fat on it will prevent the cake from rising well.

Separate eggs directly from the refrigerator, then cover them tightly and let them warm to room temperature before beating. (Eggs separate more easily when cold but the whites beat to greater volume when they are between 60 and 70 degrees.) When separating eggs, use 2 small bowls, transferring each successfully separated white to a large bowl. If a trace of yolk slips in to the whites, the whole lot will not attain maximum volume.

The yolks, beaten lightly with a pinch of salt and put into small airtight containers marked with quantity, will keep in a freezer for 9 months. Or use them in recipes requiring extra yolks such as Kulich and Pashka.

Sift together flour and half of the sugar 4 times and set aside. Add salt to the egg whites and beat until just frothy, then add cream of tartar. Beat until egg whites are stiff but not dry. Add the vanilla and almond extract. Sift the remaining sugar directly onto the egg whites while folding in lightly with a spatula.

Gently fold in the sifted flour and sugar mixture a little at a time. Turn into an *ungreased* 10-inch tube pan and bake in the lower third of a 350 degree oven for 40 to 45 minutes or until cake tester comes out dry.

Turn the cake upside down, resting the center tube over the neck of a bottle. Let it rest undisturbed for 1½ hours.

This cake is lovely as is, or frost with Rose Icing for a spectacular presentation.

Rose Icing

This icing, made from egg whites and powdered sugar, is also called Royal Icing. With a processor it is a snap to produce a smooth, satiny consistency. Rose water for flavoring is an antique conceit—and a perfect flowery touch for a garden party. Old recipes specify from as little as a teaspoon to as much as a tablespoon of rose water. Warning—rose essence, a concentrate, is not the same as rose water. If using essence, one drop—or two for the daring—is ample. Any more would incline one to rub the frosting on the hands, rather than eat it.

    2 cups confectionery sugar, sifted
    2 egg whites, at room temperature
    1 to 2 drops rose essence or 1 teaspoon rose water
    1 teaspoon almond extract
    Pinch of salt
    Few drops of red food coloring

Place egg whites in food processor. Or, if using an electric mixer, place them in a small deep bowl. While mixing or processing, slowly add the sifted confectionery sugar. When all sugar has been added, add rose flavoring, almond extract, salt and a few drops of food coloring. (The icing will have a grayish cast if it is not tinted.) Continue mixing until the icing becomes stiff and creamy. Spread on cake. Icing will harden as it sits. Mixing too long may warm the icing, making it runny. If this happens, cover tightly with plastic wrap and chill until consistency firms.

Trim cake top with candied flower petals, or just before serving, scatter a few fresh rose petals on top. This cake deserves to be presented on a lace doily on a pedestal cake plate.

Petit Fours

Petit Four foolery reached a zenith with the French pastry chefs—one book solemnly lists hundreds of different varieties, each with their official requirements. For example: Hellines, kidney-shaped, soaked in anisette liqueur, coated with anisette-flavored pink icing, adorned with crystallized pineapple; Marquises, squares filled with chocolate heaped up to form a pyramid, coated with violet-colored icing and adorned with pistachio; Indianas, cocoa and almond fingers iced in a checkerboard design.

Petit Fours should be small enough to be eaten in two mouthfuls. Ground nuts, especially pistachios for their brilliant green color, candied fruit, sugared petals (especially violets) and chocolate curls are proper and popular trimmings. Guests always say, "Too beautiful to eat," as they nibble one after another. A recipe for Crystallized Flowers is given on page 134.

The Cake

This cake is a pound cake type. It has a fine crumb and is easy to handle and ice. It will make two 8-inch square cakes which cut up into a total of 50 Petit Fours.

1 cup butter
1 cup sugar
6 eggs, at room temperature
1 teaspoon vanilla
2¼ cups cake flour

Beat butter until creamy. Add sugar and beat until mixture is light and fluffy. Beat in eggs, one at a time, whipping each fast for three minutes. Stir in vanilla.

Put cake flour into a sifter and, holding it directly over butter and egg mixture, sift it while folding into the batter.

Divide batter evenly into two 8-inch square pans which have been buttered and lined with buttered wax paper dusted lightly with flour.

Bake at 300 degrees for 35 minutes or until cake tester comes out dry. Cool in pans for five minutes, then turn out onto racks and peel off paper.

Fondant Icing

This classic icing for Petit Fours is sugar and water boiled to the soft-ball stage and then worked until it turns from clear liquid to a satiny white. Although approached by some cooks with trepidation, this recipe has worked the first time for absolute novices. If possible, remove children, dogs, and phone from the hook before beginning.

3 tablespoons white corn syrup
1 cup water
3 cups sugar

Put the corn syrup in a heavy saucepan and thin it with a bit of the water. Add the remainder of the water but do not stir from this point on. It is important to keep the sides of the pan free of sugar to avoid graininess. Add the sugar to the pan, place on high heat and swirl carefully while the sugar dissolves into the water. When syrup turns clear, cover the pan snugly—steam will wash down the sides of the pan—and boil rapidly for 3 minutes. Uncover and continue boiling until syrup reaches 240 degrees on a candy thermometer or when syrup dropped in cold water forms into a soft ball. Use a fresh spoon for each dip—again, to avoid graininess. If boiling is stopped before this point is reached or if the syrup is allowed to boil beyond it, successful fondant will not be produced.

Pour syrup onto marble slab or directly onto scrubbed formica counter top. Do not scrape pan. The syrup will cover an area of about 16 by 20 inches. Let it cool for 10 minutes; a crackled glaze will have formed on the surface. With a pastry scraper or a sturdy spatula begin scraping the syrup from the outside, turning it into the center. Continue this kneading as it turns from transparent to cloudy to pure white. When it becomes difficult to turn and has become a solid mass the fondant is finished. Store it in an airtight plastic container or wrap very tightly in plastic. Let it rest overnight—or at least for a few hours—before using.

Cut the edges from the cakes and with a ruler cut each 8-inch square into 5 rows across and 5 rows down. (Allowing for trimming, the individual cakes will be about 1¼-inch square.) Keep them covered with plastic wrap.

Place a cupful of fondant in a small saucepan set directly in a pan of warm water on low heat. Stir the fondant as it softens and thin it with as much water as necessary. The fondant coats so well that it must be thinner than will at first seem necessary—a few sample cakes dipped will demonstrate. The finished icing should be a glass-like glaze; globs are not acceptable. Vanilla or almond extract, rum or liqueurs may be added for flavoring.

Tint the fondant with food coloring to suit one's fancy or the party's decor. Chocolate morsels may be melted into a portion of the fondant.

Brush loose crumbs from the cake cube, tip saucepan and drop cube in. Spoon fondant over all sides, turning the cube. Remove with a toothpick to rack placed over waxed paper. Drippings of fondant, when set, may be returned to the pan and remelted.

Crystallized Flowers

Time suspended in a blue wildflower, a violet, a sprig of mint leaves. It's child's play to turn flowers or their petals into sweet and sentimental confections, using egg white and sugar.

First, collect an assortment of tiny flowers or petals. Small daisies, ageratum, a geranium floweret, and especially suitable are the wildflowers as they tend to be small and subtly colored. Almost any flower will do but don't use those grown from bulbs, as they may be poisonous.

> 1 egg white
> 2 drops of water
> Superfine granulated sugar

Beat the egg white with the water until slightly foamy. Dip the blossom in, coating it completely. A very small paint brush may help to do this. A toothpick will unfurl petals that may stick together. Tweezers will be helpful in transferring the tiniest flowers. After coating, transfer the flower to a plate spread with superfine sugar and sift more over it, making sure it is entirely coated with the sugar. Space coated flowers on paper toweling. Leave in a warm, dry spot to dry thoroughly—which may take several days. Store airtight until used.

Jam Creams

A most unusual cookie—in the British manner it would be called a biscuit. As to ingredients, it is more a miniature tart. Two rounds of short-crust pastry are double-deckered together with a tad of buttercream filling and jam. Stamped out with a scalloped cookie cutter and then pricked with a fork before baking to prevent uneven puffing, the Jam Creams are most decorative.

¾ cup butter
1½ cups flour
¼ cup cream

With an electric mixer beat the butter and the flour together until a dough forms. Add the cream and blend. Refrigerate for an hour or longer.

Rub some flour onto a sheet of waxed paper. With a rolling pin, roll the dough out on it to ¼-inch thickness. With a 2-inch scalloped cookie cooker (a ravioli stamp works perfectly) press out cookies but do not remove them from waxed paper. Place on tray in freezer for 5 to 10 minutes or just until dough stiffens. Peel cookies off paper and place on ungreased baking sheet. With a fork prick 4 even rows on each cookie. (Gather up extra dough and reroll when it has warmed to room temperature.) Bake cookies in 375 degree oven for 10 minutes or until just beginning to color.

When cool, spread with a bit of jam and butter cream and sandwich two cookies together. Makes 2 dozen.

Butter Cream

3 tablespoons butter, softened
2 tablespoons confectionery sugar
½ teaspoon vanilla

Cream butter and sugar together and stir in vanilla.

XII

Dim Sum Tea Lunch

Tea Eggs
Buns
Radish Fans
Pot Stickers
Dipping Sauces
Peanut Sauce, Sweet and Sour Sauce
Date Dumplings
Spiced Cashews
Almond Jelly
Fortune Cookies

Finally, an appropriate end to a tour of teahouses near and far is a stop on the continent of China, where it all began more than 4000 years ago. The Chinese discovered that the leaves from a wild evergreen of the camellia family made a brew strangely satisfying. That it would affect the course of civilization could not have been prophesied even by so wise a man as Confucius. The tea trade, nurtured by the graceful Clipper Ships, brought the farthest reaches of the globe closer; tea's rarity brought on the Revolutionary War.

A visit to a Dim Sum Teahouse reminds us that Marco Polo was the first westerner to taste dumplings and noodles. Seven centuries ago he carried them home to Italy where they were welcomed enthusiastically and renamed ravioli and pasta.

The Dim Sum Teahouse serves from morning to late afternoon. Tiered trolleys crowded with dumplings in dazzling variety are wheeled among the customers. Choices are made and sampled with friends, along with cup after cup of tea. The tea lunch is a very sociable time of shared food, news and gossip. At the end, the bill is reckoned by counting up the small empty plates.

Dim Sum translated means dot heart or touch the heart—another example of food served with tea that comforts more than the belly. In a way, the dumpling is to the Chinese what the sandwich is to the rest of the world. Dumplings may be steamed, fried or baked—or a combination of these methods. Fillings are of infinite number: pork or shrimp, sprouts or scallions, or sweet ingredients such as bean paste, dates and nuts. The dough, folded, twisted and swirled into distinctive shapes, is artistry in wrapping.

Gracious manners are reflected in the way tea is served. Both hands are used when passing or accepting a tea cup; it is considered slovenly to use only one hand. The spout of the teapot must never be pointed in the direction of a guest—an omen that a quarrel will occur.

There are so many intriguing teas from China that it is difficult to decide which to serve. Jasmine is an excellent choice. It is oolong tea with real jasmine blossoms added. When the boiling water is poured over them, the petals release the heady aroma of jasmine. Or savor the subtleties of one of the green teas. Notable is Green Gunpowder. It ought to be brewed up, like jasmine, with the leaves fully visible as they put on a fine performance. The leaves are a silvery green, rolled into tight round balls—hence the name gunpowder. The boiling water uncurls the balls into flat, surprisingly large leaves. This tea is low in caffeine, is slightly astringent and may be the world's oldest tea. One of the most precious of the green teas is the famous Dragon Well. It is grown in Hangzhou, a high valley surrounded by mountains. The choicest leaves are picked and dried by hand and its flavor is so prized that it is used at times as a spice. But not for all the tea in China should milk, lemon or sugar be allowed to intrude into the steaming purity of fine Chinese tea.

The following menu, although authentic, is simple enough for a novice to prepare. A group of "Yankee Devils" might enjoy preparing the dishes together, for as Confucius said, "Many hands make light work."

The occasion for a Dim Sum Tea Lunch? There are many— perhaps to celebrate The Feast of Excited Insects, The Rats' Wedding Day, The Festival of The Hungry Ghosts or The Moon's Birthday—or simply to dot the hearts of good friends.

Tea Eggs

With a tracery of color marbling them, Tea Eggs look like the eggs of a rare bird. They are made by crackling all over—but not removing—the shells from hard-boiled eggs which are then steeped in a brew of tea leaves, spices and seasonings. With a tang of soy and anise flavoring they are as tasty as they are lovely to look at. Small-sized eggs, if they are available, add to the effect. Quail eggs are best of all.

Start these at least one day ahead as they need to steep for 24 hours.

    1 dozen small eggs
    2 tablespoons salt
    2 tablespoons soy sauce
    4 pieces star anise (or 1 tablespoon crushed anise seed)
    2 tablespoons loose black tea leaves (or 3 tea bags)
    Spinach or parsley for garnish

With a pin prick a hole in the broad end of each egg to help prevent cracking while cooking. Place eggs in pan and cover with water. When water boils, turn down heat and let eggs simmer for 10 minutes. Drain pot and refill with cold water. After one minute, drain off water and tap each egg all over lightly on counter until shells are completely networked with cracks—but do not remove shells.

Put eggs back in pan and cover with cold water. Add salt, soy sauce, anise and tea leaves and bring to a boil. Lower the heat, cover and simmer for 2 hours. Remove from heat, cool and refrigerate in the liquid for at least 24 hours before serving.

Tea eggs may be served warm or cold. To serve warm, simply heat to warm through. Either way, just before serving, peel. Dry eggs with a paper towel and arrange on plate garnished with spinach leaves or parsley or other salad greenery. For a variety of shades, dip a few of the shelled eggs back into the brew briefly to color them all over.

Buns

They are so highly esteemed in the cuisine of China and so woven into folk tradition that a Bun Festival is held each year. Buns may be filled with meats or sweets or served plain. They may be simple fat rounds or formed into imaginative shapes—butterflies, flowers or animals. Frequently Buns are steamed using tiered or nested layers made from bamboo or metal. This recipe has been developed for oven steaming. It requires no steaming equipment, avoids the pitfalls of wrinkling or heaviness (alas, for the Buns and not the cook) and provides some leeway in holding time. This recipe includes directions for filling the Buns with red bean paste—which makes them a distant relative of our jelly doughnuts. Red bean paste in cans is easily located in large supermarkets or Oriental food shops.

   3 tablespoons sugar
   1½ teaspoons dry yeast
   1 cup warm water (115 degrees)
   3 cups flour
   1 tablespoon lard, melted—or vegetable oil, preferably peanut
   1 teaspoon baking powder
   Red bean paste
   Red food color

Dissolve sugar with yeast in warm water in a small bowl. Measure flour directly onto board. Stir lard or oil into yeast mixture. Form a well in the center of the flour and with a wooden spoon (or chopsticks) stir the liquid into it. Knead dough 15 minutes or until it becomes smooth and stretchy, adding more flour to the board if needed.

Knead dough into a ball and turn to coat in a greased bowl. Cover with damp kitchen towel and let rise in warm place for 2 to 3 hours or until almost tripled in size.

Punch down dough. Sprinkle on the baking powder gradually while kneading thoroughly on lightly floured board. Form into a long loaf and then slice down the center lengthwise forming 2 long logs. With a knife, slice into 1-inch pieces, making 2 dozen Buns. Keep covered with damp towel while shaping.

If filling buns, portion out 24 teaspoons of bean paste on a sheet of waxed paper. Knead each piece of dough into a round, flat circle. Place bean paste in center and pinch edges of dough together tightly to seal. As the object is to have the paste centered in the bun, try to keep the amount of pinched-together dough minimal.

As buns are formed place in deep pans (2½ to 3 inches high) leaving 2 inches of space between each. Keep covered with damp towel.

When all are formed they may be marked in the traditional way with a red imprint in the center. Use the end of a chopstick or a drinking straw that has been dipped in red food coloring.

Let buns rise in a warm place until doubled in size—about 45 minutes. Replace damp towel with tight fitting lid or cover tightly with foil. The moisture in the dough will provide just enough steam. Bake at 350 degrees for 30 minutes. The Buns should be smooth and white on the outside but thoroughly baked inside. They may be held in the oven, covered, with heat set on warm, for up to ½ hour. If baked ahead, they may be reheated just before serving. Makes 2 dozen.

Radish Fans

Find a bunch of fresh, fat radishes for this attractive garnish—which also serves as a beginner's introduction to the fine Oriental art of vegetable cutting.

Trim both ends off the radish. Place two chopsticks flat on a cutting board and firmly anchor the radish lengthwise between them. With a small, sharp knife, cut the radish across in thin, even slices. The chopsticks will prevent the knife from cutting all the way through the radish skin and will provide uniformity. The result will be a delicate fan. Spread the cut radishes out in various shapes and hold open with a toothpick inserted through the center. Refrigerate in ice water until shapes are set. To serve, drain, pat dry and arrange on plate on washed radish leaves.

Pot Stickers

These are fat, filled dumplings that are first fried until their bottoms brown, then covered and steamed. Packaged dough wrappers are available fresh or frozen and come in squares or circles. They are called won ton, spring roll or egg roll wrappers—the latter are thicker and make for heavier dumplings. This recipe makes about 2 dozen, but the recipe may easily be halved.

½ pound lean ground pork (or 2 pork chops, minced finely)
½ cup Chinese celery or Chinese cabbage, chopped
3 slices ginger root, minced
1 tablespoon scallion, chopped
1 tablespoon soy sauce
1 tablespoon dry sherry
1 tablespoon oil (preferably sesame or peanut)
½ teaspoon salt
½ teaspoon pepper
24 round wrappers (3-inch size)
2 tablespoons oil for frying

Combine pork, vegetable, ginger root, scallion, soy sauce, sherry, 1 tablespoon oil, salt and pepper, and let stand 15 minutes to allow flavor to develop. In a hot skillet, toss the mixture briefly just until pork loses its pinkness. Turn out onto plate.

Remove one wrapper at a time (thawed, if using frozen), keeping others covered so they will not dry out.

Place 1 tablespoon of filling on the dumpling wrapper. Gather edges up around the filling, pleating and pinching them at the top so that dumpling resembles an open marble bag. The filling should be visible at the top.

In a heavy skillet heat 2 tablespoons oil until hot. Reduce heat to medium. In two or more batches, fry dumplings until bottoms are golden. Arrange all bottom-browned dumplings in a very large skillet and pour in 1 cup of boiling water. Immediately cover tightly and steam over high heat for 2 minutes. Reduce heat to medium high and steam until most of the liquid has been absorbed and dumpling dough is tender. Unstick the Pot Stickers from the skillet with a spatula. Serve hot.

Dipping Sauces

A bowl of Dipping Sauce—usually a sweet and sour variation—is a good accompaniment for dumplings. These two can be prepared in minutes.

Peanut Sauce
3 tablespoons oil, preferably sesame or peanut
3 tablespoons smooth peanut butter
1 small clove garlic, mashed and minced finely
1 teaspoon white vinegar
2 tablespoons soy sauce
1 tablespoon orange juice

Blend oil with peanut butter to make a smooth paste. Then stir in garlic, vinegar, soy sauce and orange juice until well blended.

Sweet and Sour Sauce

3 tablespoons ketchup
2 tablespoons sugar
3 tablespoons water
1 tablespoon white vinegar
1 teaspoon soy sauce
½ teaspoon salt
1 teaspoon oil, preferably sesame or peanut
1 teaspoon cornstarch dissolved in 2 teaspoons water

In a saucepan combine all of the ingredients. Bring to a boil over moderately high heat, stirring. Simmer a few minutes until sauce turns clear and has thickened slightly. Serve hot or cold.

Date Dumplings

1 cup dates, pitted and chopped
½ cup chopped walnuts
Grated rind of 1 lemon
2 tablespoons orange juice
24 square dumpling wrappers (see page 143)
Oil for deep frying

Combine the dates, walnuts, grated lemon rind and orange juice and knead well together. Add more orange juice if mixture is too dry to hold together. Form into cylinders using a tablespoon of filling and rolling it between the palms of the hands.

Place date cylinder diagonally across the wrapper, just below center. Bring the point over the filling and roll up. Fasten the outside point by moistening with water. Put a finger into each end of the roll and twist it to seal the ends—it will look like a party-favor cracker.

Deep fry the dumplings, a few at a time, in oil heated to 375 degrees. Turn them occasionally until they are browned and crisp—a few minutes. Drain on paper towels. Makes 24.

Spiced Cashews

This recipe is offered as a bow to the Chinese custom of serving contrasting tastes and textures within a meal. In this dish, the crunch of the nuts plays well against the chewy tangerine bits. If cashews are unavailable, raw peanuts may be substituted. Five Spice Powder, a common Chinese spice blend, may be purchased or a good facsimile made by mixing together ½ teaspoonsful of ground anise, cinnamon, cloves, ginger and black pepper.

> 1 tangerine peel
> 1 tablespoon sugar
> 1 cup raw cashews (about ½ pound)
> 2 teaspoons oil
> 1 tablespoon Five Spice Powder
> ¼ teaspoon salt

Remove the peel from a tangerine and with a small, sharp knife scrape off the inside white layer. Cut the rind into slivers. Over low heat melt the sugar in a small saucepan with the tangerine shreds.

Meanwhile, stir-fry the cashews with the oil in a skillet. Sprinkle with Five Spice Powder and salt and stir well. Finally add tangerines and sugar syrup and stir to coat nuts well. Store airtight.

Almond Jelly

This is a rare dessert from old China. The original recipe called for ground almonds and agar, the gelatin from the sea. Almond extract and powdered gelatin are commonly used now, but the smooth texture and delicate flavor remain the same. Cut the jelly into cubes or the traditional diamond shapes. Guests will find that eating them with chopsticks is an amusing challenge.

> 1½ cups cold water
> 2 envelopes unflavored gelatin
> 1 cup sugar
> 1½ cups milk
> 1 tablespoon almond extract
> Kumquats or kiwis

Put water into a saucepan. Sprinkle gelatin evenly over the surface and allow to soften for five minutes. Stirring constantly, bring to a boil over medium heat to dissolve gelatin. Remove from heat. Add sugar and stir until dissolved. Then stir in milk and almond extract. Pour into an 8-inch square pan and refrigerate for 3 hours or overnight.

When firm, cut into cubes or diamond shapes. Transfer to serving dish. The jellies look especially festive when garnished with circles sliced from kumquats or fresh kiwis. Cut into 25 cubes or 18 diamonds.

Fortune Cookies

Those unauthentic and slightly absurd but absolutely essential endings to a Chinese restaurant meal are easy—and fun—to bake at home. Personalized messages may be directed to certain guests, or fill the cookies with solemn inanities from the list which follows and distribute them to guests willy-nilly.

Since these must be folded and shaped very quickly before they cool, bake them one at a time. When cookie has been formed, prop it between a rock and a hard place until it has cooled and set its shape.

¼ cup flour
¼ cup cornstarch
¼ cup sugar
¼ teaspoon salt
¼ cup vegetable oil
2 egg whites
2 teaspoons lemon juice
1 teaspoon vanilla

Sift together into a bowl the flour, cornstarch, sugar and salt. Blend in oil. Add egg whites, lemon juice and vanilla and beat until smooth.

Drop a heaping teaspoon of batter in the center of a baking sheet and spread it into a 3-inch circle. Bake in 325 degree oven for 10 to 12 minutes or until edges begin to brown.

With spatula loosen cookie from baking sheet. Fold the cookie into a half-circle, pinching it together at the top of the curved sides. Do not crease the straight side into a fold but push it forward while bringing the two ends together until they almost meet. Prop until cool so that cookie will not uncurl. The fortune slip may be placed on the center of the cookie before folding or it may be tucked in afterward. Makes at least 1 dozen.

Fortune Classics

There will be no harm in asking
You are in good hands for the time being
Press your advantage; shine your shoes
Remember your mother's advice!
Remember your mother's advice?
You are secretly being admired
Keep talking, success is near
Soft shoulders ahead
You will benefit from tonight's experience
A secret admirer will soon expose himself
Ignore all previous fortunes

A Few Kitchen Weights, Measures, and Metric Equivalents

Metric conversions don't always work out in tidy round numbers because one must deal with decimals. For examples, to convert ounces to grams, you multiply ounces by 28.35. However, the following simple tables give accepted equivalents for many of the quantities and ingredients used in this book, should you wish to experiment with the metric system.

		liquid	*approximate* *grams*
60 drops	1 teaspoon	$\frac{1}{6}$ oz.	
3 teaspoons	1 tablespoon	$\frac{1}{2}$ oz.	15 g.
4 tablespoons	$\frac{1}{4}$ oz.	2 oz.	60 g.
16 tablespoons	1 cup	8 oz.	225 g.
2 cups	1 pint	16 oz.	450 g. (1 lb.)
4 cups	1 quart	32 oz.	900 g. (2 lbs.)

Temperatures, Fahrenheit to Celsius

225 degrees F	110 degrees C
250 degrees F	120 degrees C
300 degrees F	150 degrees C
350 degrees F	180 degrees C
375 degrees F	190 degrees C

Inches to Centimeters

1 inch	2.5 cm
1½ inches	4 cm
3 inches	8 cm
8 inches	20 cm

Sugar

2 tablespoons granulated (1 oz.)	25-30 g.
1 cup granulated	200 g.
2 cups granulated (1 lb.)	450 g.
1 cup confectionery	115 g.
3⅓ cups confectionery (1 lb.)	450 g.

Flour

½ cup (2½ oz.)	70 g.
1 cup	140 g.
3¾ cups (1 lb.)	450 g.

Butter

1 oz. (¼ stick)	2 tablespoons	30 g.
1 cup (2 sticks, ½ lb.)	16 tablespoons	225 g.
2 cups (1 lb.)	32 tablespoons	450 g.

Chocolate and Cocoa*

1 square unsweetened	1 oz.	30 g.
1 cup semisweet morsels	6 oz.	170-180 g.
1 cup cocoa	4 oz.	115 g.

*To substitute for 1 square unsweetened chocolate, use 3 tablespoons (approximately 22 g., ¾ oz.) cocoa plus 1 tablespoon (30 g., ½ oz.) butter.

Eggs

1 egg yolk	1 tablespoon
1 "large" egg	2 tablespoons
5 whole eggs	1 cup

Apples

3 medium	1 lb.	450 g.
1 cup chopped	4 oz.	115 g.

Glossary of Teatime Terms

Biscuits   British cookies.

Caddy   a small, ornate box for storing tea leaves.

Cambric tea   a children's beverage of warm milk lightly colored with tea.

Compote   a long stemmed dish.

Cozy   a padded cover placed over teapot to keep it warm.

Cream Tea   basic English tea fare—a pot of tea, scones, strawberry jam, butter—with the addition of clotted or heavy whipped cream.

Crumpets   small round yeast cakes riddled with holes.

Curate   a three-legged stand with three round shelves just big enough for one plate. Sometimes called a cake stand.

Dumbwaiter   a portable serving table formed by a center pedestal surrounded by three circular shelves.

Fool   puréed fruit mixed with whipped cream.

High tea   a light supper with a menu featuring at least one hot dish or savory and a variety of breads and cakes.

Kettle   the spouted, covered pot used to bring water to a boil.

Nippy   the name once selected via a nationwide contest for the white-aproned waitresses of old English tea rooms.

Paper cases fluted paper cups—sometimes printed with colored flowers—in various sizes used for baking or for serving sweets.

Pasty a pastry circle folded over various savory fillings. Rhymes with nasty.

Ratafia tiny cookies made and flavored with almonds.

Samovar an urn with a spigot used to boil water. Originally fueled with charcoal.

Savory any dish that is not sweet, often made with cheese.

Scones soft pastry generously fluffed with leavening. The Scotch pronounce it to rhyme with fawns.

Slop basin a pot used to hold the water discarded after warming the teapot.

Spirit burner a table-top heating device fueled by alcohol. Also called spirit lamp.

Tart pans baking pans also called teacake, gem, tartlet and patty pans.

Tea ball a small, perforated metal ball used to contain tea leaves while immersed in boiling water. Also called an infusor.

Tea gown a special dress worn by the hostess of days past. Made of soft fabric with flowing sleeves and a train, it was halfway between a ball gown and a negligée.

Tea service a set of matching china cups, saucers, plates and tea pot.

Tongs   a utensil used to dispense sugar cubes.

Trifle   a sweet made of spongecake, jam, custard, whipped cream and sherry.

Trolley   a small table on wheels, also called a tea cart.

Varieties of Tea

Green

Basket Fired   Kangra
China Green   Pan Fried
Dragon Well   Young Hyson
Gunpowder

Oolong

Formosa Oolong
Pouchong (blended or scented with jasmine or gardenia blossoms)

Black

Assam   Keemum
Ceylon (Sri Lanka)   Lapsang Souchong
Darjeeling

Blended

Earl Grey   Queen Mary
English Breakfast   Royal
Irish Breakfast   Russian Style
Lady Londonderry

Flavored and Spiced

Apple   Orange Spice
Cinnamon   Strawberry

Herbal and Special

Beef   Lavender
Cambric   Lemon Verbena
Camomile   Mint
Catnip   Rose Hip
Ginseng

Bibliography

These books supplied much of the background material for this book.

Beeton, Isabella. *Mrs. Beeton's Book of Household Management.* London: Ward Lock, 1899.

Craig, Elizabeth. *Court Favourites, Recipes From Royal Kitchens.* London: Andre Deutsch, 1953.

Francatelli, Charles Elmé. *Francatelli's Modern Cook.* London: Bentley, 1846.

McNeill, Florence Marian. *The Scots Kitchen.* London: Blackie and Son, Ltd., 1929.

Schapira, Joel, David and Karl. *The Book of Coffee & Tea.* New York: St. Martin's Press, 1975.

Ukers, William. *All About Tea.* New York: Tea and Coffee Trade Journal, 1935.

Index

Albert, Prince, 8
Almond Jelly, 147
Angel Cake, 129–130
Apple:
  Cake, Fresh, 26–27
  Charlotka, 64–65
  Kisel, 62
  metric conversions for, 151
Apricot:
  Charlotka, 64–65
  in Chocolate Gold, 29
  Sugar Plums, 16–18
Asparagus Rolls, 126–127

Baking powder, 1
Basin, slop, 153
Battenberg Cake, 12–13
Beef Tea, 49
Biscuits, 152
Black Bread, 66–67
  caramel color for, 67
Black Bun, 94–96
  filling for, 95
  pastry for, 95
Black tea, 3, 155
Blended tea, 3, 9, 155
Bourbon Balls, 106
Boxties, 119
Brandy Snaps, 80
Bread:
  Black, 66–67
  Chocolate, 127–128
  hand mixing for, 75–76
  Kulich, 58–59
  Oatmeal, 89
  processor mixing for, 76–77
  Sally Lunn, 39

  Soda, 114–115
  White, 74–77
  Whole Wheat, 77
Bread and Butter Pudding, 51
Brown Sugar Bears, 52–53
Bun, Black, 94–96
Buns, 141–142
  Hot Cross, 41
  Pumpkin, 50
Butter, 1
  cream, 135
  metric conversions for, 151
  Pudding, Bread and, 51
  Rum, 115
  Vanilla, 128
Butterscotch, 99

Caddy, 152
Cake:
  Angel, 129–130
  Apple, Fresh, 26–27
  Battenberg, 12–13
  Black Bun, 94–96
  Chocolate, 84–85
  Porter, 116–117
  Zebra, 53
Cakes, tea:
  Crumpets, 10–11
  Mazurkas, 63
  potato (Boxties), 119
  Seedcake, 40
Cambric tea, 152
Candied Fruits, 70–71
Candy, Butterscotch, 99
Caramel color, 67
Cashews, Spiced, 146
Celsius, Fahrenheit converted to, 150

Centimeters, inches converted to, 150
Charlotka, 64–65
Cheese:
    Love Letters, 81
    Pashka, 59–61
    Rarebit, 36–37
Cherry Tarts (Cupid's Love Wells), 14–15
Chinese Buns, 141–142
Chocolate:
    Bread, 127–128
    Cake, 84–85
    Gold, 29
    metric conversions for, 151
    Petit Fours, 131–134
    Soup, 48
Cigarettes Russes, 28
Cinnamon Toast, Real, 78–79
Clotted Cream, 94
Cocoa, metric conversions for, 151
Compote, 152
Cookies:
    Apricot Sugar Plums, 16–18
    Bourbon Balls, 106
    Brown Sugar Bears, 52–53
    Cigarettes Russes, 28
    Fortune, 148–149
    Gingerbread Husbands, 98
    Graham Crackers, 147
    Jumbles, 42–43
    Lady's Navel, 33
    Lips of the Beauty, 32–33
    Oatmeal, 120
    Poppyseed, 27
    Ratafias, 19, 153
    Trilbys, 82–83
Cornish Pasties, 37–38
    filling for, 38
    pastry for, 38
Cozy, 152
Cranberries:
    Candied, 70
    Kisel, 62
Cream, Clotted, 94

Cream Patties, 79
Cream Puffs, 106–108
    fillings for, 108
Creams, Jam, 135
Cream tea, 152
Crumpets, 10–11, 152
Crystallized Flowers, 134
Cucumber Sandwiches, 103
Cupid's Love Wells, 14–15
Curate, 152

Date Dumplings, 145
Dim Sum tea lunch, 137–149
Dipping Sauces, 144–145
Dumbwaiter, 152
Dumplings:
    Date, 145
    filled (Pot Stickers), 143–144

Eggs, 1
    Mazurkas, 63
    Meringue Mushrooms, 68–69
    metric conversions for, 151
    Pashka, 59–61
    Scots, 91
    Tea, 149
    Woodcock, 92

Fabergé, Carl, 56
Fahrenheit converted to Celsius, 150
Fancy Sandwiches, 125–127
Farina Pudding, 57
Fish House Punch, 110–111
Flavored and spiced tea, 155
Flour, 1
    metric conversions for, 151
Flowers, Crystallized, 134
    Petit Fours with, 131–134
Fondant icing, 132–134
Fool, 152
    Gooseberry, 111
Fortune Cookies, 148–149
    classic fortunes for, 149
Francatelli, Charles, 14

Fruit, in Black Bun, 94–96
Fruit and Nut Balls, 29
Fruits, Candied, 70–71
  Cranberries, 70
  Pears, 71
  Petit Fours, 131–134

Garden party, 123–135
Gingerbread Husbands, 98
Glossary, of teatime terms, 152–154
Gooseberry Fool, 111
Gown, tea, 153
Graham Crackers, 47
Green tea, 3, 155
Gypsy tea room, 23–33

Hand mixing, for bread, 75–76
Hearthside tea in Irish kitchen, 121
Herbal and special tea, 155
High tea, 35–43, 152
Honey:
  Mazurkas, 63
  and Nut Puffs, 30–31
Hot Cross Buns, 41

Icing:
  fondant, 132–134
  Rose, 130–131
Inches converted to centimeters, 150
Ingredients, 1
Irish kitchen, hearthside tea in, 113–121

Jam:
  Plum, 116
  Strawberry, 11
Jam Creams, 135
  butter cream for, 135
Jelly, Almond, 147
Jelly Rolls, 108–109
Johnson, Samuel, 87
Jumbles, 42–43
  glaze for, 43

Kettle, 152

Kisel, 61–62
  Apple, 62
  Cranberry, 62
  Pour, 61
  Spoon, 62
Kulich, 58–59
  icing for, 59

Ladies Home Journal, 8
Lady's Navel, 33
Lemon Curd Tartlets, 117–119
  curd for, 117–118
  pastry for, 118–119
Lips of the Beauty, 32–33
Love Letters, 81

McKinley, William, 8
Madeleines, 104–105
Marmalade, Orange, 90
Marzipan, 13
Mazurkas, 63
Measures, 150–151
Meat Pies (Cornish Pasties), 37–38
Meringue Mushrooms, 68–69
Metric equivalents, 150–151
Mixing:
  hand, for bread, 75–76
  processor, for bread, 76–77

Nippy, 152
Nursery tea, 45–53
Nut Balls, with Fruit, 29
Nut Puffs, Honey and, 30–31
  filling for, 30
  syrup for, 30–31
Nuts:
  Cashews, Spiced, 146
  Chocolate Bread, 127–128
  Petit Fours, 131–134
  Spiced, 110

Oatmeal:
  Bread, 89
  Cookies, 120

Oolong tea, 3, 155
Orange Marmalade, 90
Oven temperature, 1

Pans, tart, 153
Paper cases, 153
Pashka, 59–61
Pasties, Cornish, 37–38
Pasty, 153
Patties, Cream, 79
Peanut Sauce, 144
Pears, Candied, 71
Petit Fours, 131–134
    cake for, 132
    Crystallized Flowers for, 134
    fondant icing for, 132–134
Petticoat Tails, 97
Pinwheel Sandwiches, 126
Plum Jam, 116
Polo, Marco, 138
Poppyseed Cookies, 27
Porter Cake, 116–117
Post, Emily, 102
Potato cakes (Boxties), 119
Pot Stickers, 143–144
Pour Kisel, 61
Procedures, standard operating, 1
Processor mixing, for bread, 76–77
Pudding:
    Bread and Butter, 51
    Farina, 57
Pumpkin Buns, 50
Punch, Fish House, 110–111

Radish:
    Fans, 143
    Sandwiches, 103–104
Raisins, in Chocolate Gold, 29
Rarebit, 36–37
Ratafias, 19, 153
Ribbon Sandwiches, 125–126
Rolls:
    Asparagus, 126–127
    Jelly, 108–109

Rose Icing, 130–131
Rum:
    Butter, 115
    Nicky, 42
Russes, Cigarettes, 28
Russian Easter tea, 55–71

Sally Lunn, 39
Salmon Sandwiches, Smoked, 104
Samovar, 153
Sandwiches, 102–104
    Cucumber, 103
    Fancy, 125–127
    Pinwheel, 126
    Radish, 103–104
    Ribbon, 125–126
    Salmon, Smoked, 104
    Tomato, 48–49
    Watercress, 78
Sauces, Dipping, 144–145
    Peanut, 144
    Sweet and Sour, 145
Savory, 153
Scones, 92–93, 153
Scotland, breakfast in, 87–99
Scots Eggs, 91
Scott, Sir Walter, 88
Seedcake, 40
Shortbread, 97
    Petticoat Tails, 97
Slop basin, 153
Snaps, Brandy, 80
Soda Bread, 114–115
Soup, Chocolate, 48
Special and herbal tea, 155
Spiced and flavored tea, 155
Spiced Cashews, 146
Spiced Nuts, 110
Spirit burner, 153
Spongecake:
    Madeleines, 104–105
    Trifle, 20–21, 154
Spoon Kisel, 62
Strawberry Jam, 11

Sugar, metric conversions for, 151
Sugar Plums, Apricot, 16–18
  cookie glue for, 17
  cookies for, 16–17
  filling for, 16–17
  glaze for, 17–18
Sweet and Sour Sauce, 145
Sweetmeats, 29

Tartlets, Lemon Curd, 117–119
Tart pans, 153
Tarts:
  Cherry, 14–15
  Rum Nicky, 42
Tea:
  blends of, 3, 9, 155
  perfect brewing of, 2–5
  serving or taking of, 4–5, 9
  for two, 73–85
  varieties of, 3, 155
Tea ball, 153
Tea cakes, see Cakes, tea
Tea dance, 101–111
Tea Eggs, 140
Tea gown, 153
Tea leaves, reading of, 24–26
Tea lunch (Dim Sum), 137–149
Tea service, 153
Teatime terms, 152–154

Temperature:
  metric conversions for, 150
  oven, 1
Terms, teatime, 152–154
Toast, Real Cinnamon, 78–79
Toffee (Yellowman), 121
Tomato Sandwiches, 48–49
Tongs, 154
Trifle, 20–21, 154
Trilbys, 82–83
Trolley, 154

Vanilla, 1
  Butter, 128
Victoria, Queen of England, tea with, 7–9

Watercress Sandwiches, 78
Weights, 150–151
White Bread, 74–77
  hand mixing for, 75–76
  processor mixing, 76–77
Whole Wheat Bread, 77
Wind in the Willows, 46
Woodcock, 92

Yeast, 1
Yellowman, 121

Zebra Cake, 53